T
PASSION
TRANSLATION

THE PASSIONATE LIFE BIBLE STUDY SERIES

12-LESSON STUDY GUIDE

THE BOOK OF
ACTS

To the Lovers of God

tPt

BroadStreet
PUBLISHING

BroadStreet Publishing® Group, LLC
Savage, Minnesota, USA
BroadStreetPublishing.com

TPT: The Book of Acts: 12-Lesson Bible Study Guide
Copyright © 2024 BroadStreet Publishing Group

9781424567645 (softcover)
9781424567652 (e-book)

Stock or custom editions of BroadStreet Publishing titles may be purchased in bulk for educational, business, ministry, fundraising, or sales promotional use. For information, please email info@broadstreetpublishing.com.

General editor: Brian Simmons
Managing editor: William D. Watkins
Writer: William D. Watkins

Design and typesetting | garborgdesign.com

Printed in China

24 25 26 27 28 5 4 3 2 1

Contents

From God's Heart to Yours

"God is love," says the apostle John, and "Everyone who loves is fathered by God and experiences an intimate knowledge of him" (1 John 4:7). The life of a Christ-follower is, at its core, a life of love—God's love of us, our love of him, and our love of others and ourselves because of God's love for us.

And this divine love is reliable, trustworthy, unconditional, other-centered, majestic, forgiving, redemptive, patient, kind, and more precious than anything else we can ever receive or give. It characterizes each person of the Trinity—Father, Son, and Holy Spirit—and so is as limitless as they are. They love one another with this eternal love, and they reach beyond themselves to us, created in their image with this love.

How do we know such incredible truths? Through the primary source of all else we know about the one God—his Word, the Bible. Of course, God reveals who he is through other sources as well, such as the natural world, miracles, our inner life, our relationships (especially with him), those who minister on his behalf, and those who proclaim him to us and others. But the fullest and most comprehensive revelation we have of God and from him is what he has given us in the thirty-nine books of the Hebrew Scriptures (the Old Testament) and the twenty-seven books of the Christian Scriptures (the New Testament). Together, these sixty-six books present a compelling and telling portrait of God and his dealings with us.

It is these Scriptures that *The Passionate Life Bible Study Series* is all about. Through these study guides, we—the editors and writers of this series—seek to provide you with a unique and welcoming opportunity to delve more deeply into God's precious Word, encountering there his loving heart for you and all the others he loves. God wants you to know him more deeply, to love him more devoutly, and to share his heart with others more frequently and freely. To accomplish this, we have based this study guide series on The Passion Translation of the Bible, which strives to "reintroduce the passion and fire of the Bible to the English reader. It doesn't merely convey the literal meaning of words. It expresses God's passion for people and his world by translating the original, life-changing message of God's Word for modern readers." It has been created to "kindle in you a burning desire to know the heart of God, while impacting the church for years to come."[1]

In each study guide, you will find an introduction to the Bible book it covers. There you will gain information about that Bible book's authorship, date of composition, first recipients, setting, purpose, central message, and key themes. Each lesson following the introduction will take a portion of that Bible book and walk you through it so you will learn its content better while experiencing and applying God's heart for your own life and encountering ways you can share his heart with others. Along the way, you will come across a number of features we have created that provide opportunities for more life application and growth in biblical understanding.

Experience God's Heart

This feature focuses questions on personal application. It will help you live out God's Word and to bring the Bible into your world in fresh, exciting, and relevant ways.

Share God's Heart

This feature will help you grow in your ability to share with other people what you learn and apply in a given lesson. It provides guidance on using the lesson to grow closer to others and to enrich your fellowship with others. It also points the way to enabling you to better listen to the stories of others so you can bridge the biblical story with their stories.

The Backstory

This feature provides ancient historical and cultural background that illuminates Bible passages and teachings. It deals with then-pertinent religious groups, communities, leaders, disputes, business trades, travel routes, customs, nations, political factions, ancient measurements and currency...in short, anything historical or cultural that will help you better understand what Scripture says and means.

 ## Word Wealth

This feature provides definitions for and other illuminating information about key terms, names, and concepts, and how different ancient languages have influenced the biblical text. It also provides insight into the different literary forms in the Bible, such as prophecy, poetry, narrative history, parables, and letters, and how knowing the form of a text can help you better interpret and apply it. Finally, this feature highlights the most significant passages in a Bible book. You may be encouraged to memorize these verses or keep them before you in some way so you can actively hide God's Word in your heart.

 ## Digging Deeper

This feature explains the theological significance of a text or the controversial issues that arise and mentions resources you can use to help you arrive at your own conclusions. Another way to dig deeper into the Word is by looking into the life of a biblical character or another person from church history, showing how that man or woman incarnated a biblical truth or passage. For instance, Jonathan Edwards was well known for his missions work among native American Indians and for his intellectual prowess in articulating the Christian faith, Florence Nightingale for the reforms she brought about in healthcare, Irenaeus for his fight against heresy, Billy Graham for his work in evangelism, Moses for the strength God gave him to lead the Hebrews and receive and communicate the law, and Deborah for her work as a judge in Israel. This feature introduces to you figures from the past who model what it looks like to experience God's heart and share his heart with others.

The Extra Mile

While The Passion Translation's notes are extensive, sometimes students of Scripture like to explore more on their own. In this feature, we provide you with opportunities to glean more information from a Bible dictionary, a Bible encyclopedia, a reliable Bible online tool, another ancient text, and the like. Here you will learn how you can go the extra mile on a Bible lesson. And not just in study either. Reflection, prayer, discussion, and applying a passage in new ways provide even more opportunities to go the extra mile. Here you will find questions to answer and applications to make that will require more time and energy from you—if and when you have them to give.

As you can see above, each of these features has a corresponding icon so you can quickly and easily identify them.

You will find other helps and guidance through the lessons of these study guides, including thoughtful questions, application suggestions, and spaces for you to record your own reflections, answers, and action steps. Of course, you can also write in your own journal, notebook, computer document, or other resource, but we have provided you with space for your convenience.

Also, each lesson will direct you toward the introductory material and numerous notes provided in The Passion Translation. There each Bible book contains a number of aids supplied to help you better grasp God's words and his incredible love, power, knowledge, plans, and so much more. We want you to get the most out of your Bible study, especially using it to draw you closer to the One who loves you most.

Finally, at the end of each lesson you'll find a section called "Talking It Out." This contains questions and exercises for application that you can share, answer, and apply with your spouse, a friend, a coworker, a Bible study group, or any other individuals or groups who would like to walk with you through this material. As Christians, we gather together to serve, study, worship, sing, evangelize, and a host of other activities. We grow together, not just on our own. This section will give you ample opportunities to engage others with some of the content of each lesson so you can work it out in community.

We offer all of this to support you in becoming an even more faithful and loving disciple of Jesus Christ. A disciple in the ancient world was a student of her teacher, a follower of his master. Students study, and followers follow. Jesus' disciples are to sit at his feet and listen and learn and then do what he tells them and shows them to do. We have created *The Passionate Life Bible Study Series* to help you do what a disciple of Jesus is called to do.

So go.

Read God's words.

Hear what he has to say in them and through them.

Meditate on them.

Hide them in your heart.

Display their truths in your life.

Share their truths with others.

Let them ignite Jesus' passion and light in all you say and do.

Use them to help you fulfill what Jesus called his disciples to do: "Now wherever you go, make disciples of all nations, baptizing them in the name of the Father, the Son, and the Holy Spirit. And teach them to faithfully follow all that I have commanded you. And never forget that I am with you every day, even to the completion of this age" (Matthew 28:19–20).

And through all of this, let Jesus' love nourish your heart and allow that love to overflow into your relationships with others (John 15:9–13). For it was for love that Jesus came, served, died, rose from the dead, and ascended into heaven. This love he gives us. And this love he wants us to pass along to others.

Why I Love the Book of Acts

The book of Acts, the sequel to the Gospel of Luke, is a captivating narrative that chronicles the dynamic and transformative journey of the early Christian church. Often referred to as the "Acts of the Holy Spirit," this book is a source of inspiration and revelation for believers seeking a deeper understanding of the power and wisdom bestowed upon followers of Jesus.

The book of Acts holds a special place in the hearts of many, myself included. Here are some reasons why I *love* it.

The Supernatural Becomes Natural: One of the most enchanting aspects of Acts is its vivid portrayal of the supernatural becoming a natural part of the lives of believers. Miracles of healing, the raising of the dead, and other acts of divine intervention are not just confined to ancient history but are also presented as tangible experiences for those who align themselves with the teachings of Christ. The book serves as a reminder that the power of God is not a distant concept but a living force that can manifest in our lives today.

The Unhindered Gospel: Acts underscores the unstoppable nature of the gospel. Despite challenges, persecution, and opposition, the message of salvation spreads like wildfire. The book of Acts demonstrates that human limitations or external circumstances do not bind the gospel; it is the dynamic power of God bringing salvation to the ends of the earth. The resilience and unyielding force of the gospel inspires believers to share their faith boldly, knowing that God's purpose cannot be hindered.

Explosive Church Growth: Acts provides a front-row seat to witness the explosive growth of the early Christian church. From a humble gathering of one hundred twenty believers, the church expands dramatically, with over three thousand joining in a single day. This phenomenal growth is attributed to the outpouring of the Holy Spirit, transforming a small and hesitant group of believers into a powerful force for good. Acts serves as a blueprint for contemporary believers, encouraging them to anticipate and embrace growth fueled by the Holy Spirit.

Bridging Historical Gaps: The absence of Acts would leave a significant historical gap between the events of the Gospels and the writing of the New Testament epistles. This book serves as a crucial link, providing essential information about the establishment and growth of early Christian communities. It answers questions about the origins of specific churches, such as Corinth, and lays the foundation for understanding the context in which the New Testament epistles were written.

Actions Speak Louder Than Doctrines: Unlike some parts of the Bible that focus predominantly on doctrinal teachings, the book of Acts is a narrative filled with actions. It vividly illustrates the powerful expression of the Holy Spirit flowing through believers, emphasizing the importance of hearing the Word and living it out in our daily lives. Reading Acts challenges us to move beyond theological discussions and embrace a faith that is active and transformative.

In my view, the book of Acts is a treasure trove of inspiration, offering a glimpse into the Christian church's early days and the Holy Spirit's extraordinary acts. It ignites a passion for the supernatural, underscores the resilience of the gospel, and provides a historical foundation for the remaining New Testament. As we delve into the pages of Acts, we discover a timeless truth: the same Holy Spirit who empowered the early disciples is available to us today, ready to usher us into new dimensions of power and wisdom.

I know you're going to love this study guide. It has the power to ignite your heart with the flame of the Holy Spirit!

Brian Simmons
General editor

LESSON 1

Luke and His
Acts of the Apostles

(Various Scriptures)

What we know today as the book of Acts or the Acts of the Apostles is the sequel to the Gospel of Luke. The same man wrote both books. His name was Luke, and he was a traveling companion of the apostle Paul. Paul refers to him as "the beloved physician" (Colossians 4:14) and as one of his ministry companions (Philemon 24). Luke was also Paul's sole companion during his imprisonment in Rome (2 Timothy 4:11), a time when Paul thought he might be executed (vv. 6–8). Luke traveled with Paul during his second and third missionary journeys, as indicated by the switch from the author's use of "they" earlier in Acts to "we" in later chapters (Acts 16:10–17; 20:5–15; 21:1–18; 27:1–28:16). Luke's use of the first-person plural tells us when he was actually with Paul and not just describing Paul's journey using the accounts of others.

We also know that Luke was not born a Jew but a gentile, for in Colossians, Paul distinguishes between his Jewish traveling companions and his non-Jewish ones. He lists Luke among the latter group (4:10–14). As to where Luke was born and raised, we don't know. But that he wrote Acts is secured in Christian tradition along with his authorship of the Gospel that bears his name. Early church leaders such as Irenaeus (late second century), Clement of Alexandria (ca. 155–220), Tertullian (ca. 160–215), and Origen (ca. 185–254) name Luke as the author of both books. And in later centuries, his authorship of these books remained a settled matter.[2]

Luke's Gospel and Acts display an obvious connection that links them as a single work. Both books are written to Theophilus, a name that means "friend or lover of God" (Luke 1:1–4; Acts 1:1). And in both cases, the author Luke says that he is providing a reliable, trustworthy, historical account of "what Jesus accomplished and fulfilled among us" (Luke 1:1–4; cf. Acts 1).

As to the identity of this Theophilus, he may have been a historical individual, perhaps Luke's patron or a relatively new convert to Christ. Speculations abound, for all we really know about Theophilus is what Luke says about him, which isn't much. Because of this, some Bible scholars suggest that *Theophilus* stands symbolically for all who are friends or lovers of God since that is what the word *Theophilus* means. In that case, Luke's Gospel and Acts were composed for all those who love God.

Purpose of Luke-Acts

Luke's Gospel tells of Jesus' life, ministry, arrest, trials, execution, resurrection, and ascension. Acts picks up with the resurrected Jesus, Jesus giving some final instructions to his disciples, and then his ascension—events that clearly link Acts to the closing chapters of the Gospel of Luke. Then Acts begins to tell about the establishment and growth of the church, the body of Christ, including how it burst past its Jewish origins into the gentile world. Acts is the earliest history we have of the first-century church, and it takes us up to Paul preaching the gospel in Rome, the capital city of the Roman Empire.

As you can see, Acts is the second volume of a two-volume work, with the Gospel of Luke as volume 1. Both books are tied together, so the prologue of the Gospel also serves as a complement to the prologue of Acts.

- *Read Luke 1:1–4 and study note 'a' in TPT, as well as Acts 1:1 and study note 'c.' Then answer the following questions:*

  Whom did Luke address as the first recipient(s) of Luke and Acts?

  Did Luke know of other biographies of Jesus? Support your answer.

  Why did Luke choose to write his account of Jesus' life and the initial decades of the church?

  Why do such resources matter in the writing of history?

  From Luke's comments in the opening verses of his Gospel and Acts, would you say that Luke was a first-hand witness to Jesus' life, death, and resurrection, or was he a second-generation Christian writing a history of Jesus and the church? Support your answer.

Date of Acts

Determining the time when Luke wrote Acts is largely based on what that book does *not* record. Acts does not mention several events that had a major impact on the early church—events that Luke would likely have mentioned if he had not already concluded writing the book. These omitted events include the following:

- *In the spring of AD 62, the Jewish ruling body, the Sanhedrin, put to death James, the Lord's brother, without securing the permission of Roman authorities.*[3]

- *In 64, the Roman emperor Nero began to bring cruel and controversial atrocities upon Christians in the city of Rome and its surrounding districts.*[4]

- *Around the year 67, the apostles Peter and Paul were executed in Rome under the emperor Nero's reign.*[5]

- *The Zealots, a Jewish party who worked to purge Israel of its Roman overlords, led an armed revolt against the Romans from 66 to 73. The church historian Eusebius (ca. 265–339) records a tradition that, before the war against Rome began, "believers had been warned through a prophetic utterance to flee from Jerusalem to the city of Pella in Perea...Perhaps some Jerusalem believers remembered the words of Jesus (Matt. 24:15–16 [parallels Mark 13:14; Luke 21:20–21]): 'So when you see standing in the holy place "the abomination that causes desolation," spoken of through the prophet Daniel—let the reader understand—then let those who are in Judea flee to the mountains.'"[6] And Christians did flee—in droves!*

- *In the year 70, the Romans besieged Jerusalem and ultimately looted and destroyed the city and its temple. Hundreds of thousands of civilians and rebels died in the process, including children.*[7]

That Luke fails to mention any of these events indicates that he had completed writing Acts before they took place. This is especially telling for the destruction of Jerusalem and its temple in the year 70. Since Jesus had predicted their ruin (Matthew 24:1–2, 15–18; Mark 13:1–2; Luke 21:20–24), it would be incredibly odd, if not astonishing, for Luke to omit them. After all, they further confirmed Jesus' accuracy as a prophet of God.

When many scholars put these facts (and others) together, they date the writing of Acts as likely in the early 60s. If Jesus was executed in the year 33,[8] then Acts provides us with a history of the first thirty years of the Christian movement following his death, resurrection, and ascension.[9]

- *What is the value of a history of the church that was composed less than a generation after Jesus' last days on earth?*

Major Characteristics of Acts

Among the many characteristics of Acts are these:

Historical Reliability

Jesus really lived, taught, healed, performed numerous miracles, exorcised demons, faced down critics, told stories, and ended up nailed to a cross due to trumped-up charges. He was really buried in a tomb and then rose physically alive from that same tomb, showed himself alive to hundreds of witnesses over a forty-day period, and then ascended into heaven. All these things actually happened. The four Gospels present a historical record of these events, and Acts adds to them how Jesus' life and teachings, as well as his death and resurrection and ascension, became central to his early followers as they began to share his message to others and live it out themselves.

Christianity is rooted in history, in actual events, in people who really lived and followed a Savior who really lived, too, and still lives in his resurrection body. Because Christianity is historical, the New Testament writers gave us history, not just theology or wisdom, to live by. Luke is no different. His account of the early church and its growth has been repeatedly historically verified. Perhaps the most important way this occurs for ancient writings is through the work of archaeologists. They strive to confirm or challenge whether the places mentioned by ancient authors actually existed during the timeframe the writers describe. Archaeologists want to verify if the names and titles of key persons are genuine and accurate. They also want to know if the authors accurately depict the geography and if the events that the author has detailed truly occurred. For all these details and more, when Luke is put to the test, he has passed with 100 percent accuracy. Bible scholar Robert H. Gundry brings out one area of confirmed historical accuracy that was especially difficult to get right in Luke's time:

> We now know that his [Luke's] use of titles for various kinds of local and provincial governmental officials—procurators, consuls, praetors, politarchs, Asiarchs, and others—was exactly correct for the times and localities about which he was writing. The accuracy is doubly remarkable in that the usage of these terms was in a constant state of flux because the political status of various communities was constantly changing.[10]

Luke was a first-rate historian, and the findings of archaeology confirm this.[11]

- *Why does it matter that Luke paid such careful attention to detail in his writing of Acts?*

- *Do you derive any comfort from Luke's historical accuracy? Why or why not?*

The Centrality of Jesus

Luke tells us in his Gospel that he intends to provide "an orderly account of what Jesus accomplished and fulfilled among us" (Luke 1:1–4). Similarly, at the start of Acts, Luke says that he plans "to give you further details about the life of our Lord Jesus and all the things that he did and taught" (Acts 1:1). In other words, his Luke-Acts volumes center on Jesus Christ—first his earthly life and then his heavenly work through the Spirit. As the "Introduction" to Acts in *The Passion Translation* says:

> Acts opens in the same way Luke closes,
> with the ascension and exaltation of Jesus
> to the right hand of the Father. In essence,
> the disciples pick up where Jesus left off in
> seeing the salvation of the world realized.
> Not only is he the object of the church's

affection, Jesus is the content of their message! Luke makes it clear that salvation is found in no one and nothing else but Jesus and his name. The word *name* appears over fifty times in Acts, signifying that Jesus is the exalted, exclusive Lord of salvation. We are saved through him and him alone![12]

- *Christianity is Christ. Without him, there is no Christianity, no Christian church, no Christian way. Is Jesus central in your life? If so, how does he shine through?*

The Holy Spirit

One of the church fathers from the fourth century, John Chrysostom (ca. 344–407), said that "Acts is the 'gospel of the Holy Spirit' because the Spirit's presence is so evident in the book."[13] Luke refers to the Holy Spirit as "the Spirit of Jesus" in Acts 16:7. John the Baptizer had foretold that Jesus would baptize the repentant "into the Spirit of holiness and into his raging fire" (Luke 3:16). And Jesus reiterated this point when, in his resurrection state, he told the disciples that soon they would "receive the gift I told you about, the gift the Father has promised. For John baptized you in water, but in a few days from now you will be baptized in the Holy Spirit!" (Acts 1:4–5). And that baptism would show itself in "power" and enable the disciples to be Jesus' witnesses, his messengers (vv. 7–8). Acts shows how the Spirit came, what he did in and through the disciples, and how he transformed their lives and the lives of others who put their trust in Jesus Christ. Jesus is the one who sends the Spirit, and Jesus' power, direction, and message come through the Spirit's work. "The Spirit isn't reserved for the select, holy few; he is the promised gift given to all whom God has called and who believe in his Son."[14] The church's success, the fruit it bears, is the result of the work and power of the Holy Spirit.

- *Who is the Holy Spirit to you, and how would you say he manifests his work in your life?*

Salvation for All

Very early in the book of Acts, the central message of salvation is clearly stated: "Everyone who calls on the name of the Lord will be saved" (2:21). And who is the Lord that we should call on? He is Jesus, the one who was crucified. He is the one whom God the Father "made both Lord and the Messiah" (v. 36). Through the power of the Spirit, the apostle Peter said, "There is only one name to whom God has given authority by which we must experience salvation: the name of Jesus" (4:12). Acts goes on to show how this salvation message, while starting with the Jews, moved beyond them to all non-Jews, to gentiles. Salvation is open to anyone—no matter their ethnicity, nationality, social status, education, profession, gender, age, or any other distinguishing feature. Anyone who asks through faith for Jesus to save them is reconciled to God and forgiven for their sins.

- *Have you called on Jesus to deliver you from sin? Have you asked God through Jesus to have mercy on you and save you? If not, what is the reason for your hesitation?*

- *If you have been saved by Christ, spend some time right now thanking him and praising him for giving you new life and the freedom to live anew in the power of the Spirit.*

The Church

Luke's historical account in Acts shows the beginning and growth of the early church. The Greek word translated "church" is used twenty-three times in Acts, but the word, which means "gathering, assembly," doesn't capture all that the church was or is. This gathering of believers in Christ was also a community and "the Way." The church is a movement—"a Spirit-fueled movement led by leaders who articulate and apply the power of the gospel. And like most movements, the church faces opposition and persecution, yet triumphs and expands through the Holy Spirit's power."[15] Darrell Bock adds to this description of the church in Acts:

> The community itself is a place of baptism, worship, table fellowship, and instruction (...Acts 2:38–47). It is a place of prayer for the work of God (4:23–31). It also is a place where those in the church can obtain support and relief if they are materially at risk (4:32–37; 6:1–6). The Spirit guides the church in active mission to take the message to those who are not a part of the community (13:1–2).[16]

As we'll see in our study of Acts, the church was a fresh work of God that also was a fulfillment of promises that he had made long ago.

- *As a believing Christian, you are part of a movement that began two thousand years ago and continues to change the world for Christ—one person at a time. What changes do you see that have their roots in the Christian movement?*

- *Are you a change-agent for Christ? If so, in what ways do you strive to bring about change in your spheres of influence?*

Women and the Poor

Like he did in his Gospel, Luke stresses in Acts the fact that "women are fully included in Jesus' work through his community of followers. They receive the Spirit of power in full measure, empowered as witnesses of who Christ is and what he did. In some contexts, women teach and prophesy. Luke makes it clear that unlike many social contexts, women are neither dismissed nor forgotten."[17]

The same holds true for the poor. In Acts "we see the church rising up to provide for and care for them." We see Christians pooling "their resources together to care for the poor in their city."[18] We also see Christians sending food, money, and other resources to help meet the material needs of people in locales quite far away.

The church's ministry was to the soul *and* the body, to the spiritual *and* the physical. The gospel was about bringing wholeness to the whole person, not just to one's spiritual life.

- *The gospel and the church that has grown out of it, shares it, and matures in it are for all who call upon the name of the Lord for salvation. And all who become Christ's followers receive the same empowering and transforming Spirit. We may be gifted differently (1 Corinthians 12), and we may display different natural talents and skills, but all of us are equal and united in Christ (Galatians 3:26–29). In that light, how do you regard the opposite sex in the church? Do you see them as your Christian peers or as something less? How do you treat them and why?*

- *Likewise, when it comes to those of a lesser economic status than you, how do you respond to them? Are you willing to share what you have with them? Do you see their physical/material needs as important to address?*

The Defense of the Christian Faith

The apostle Peter commands Christians to "always be prepared to give an answer to everyone who asks you to give the reason for the hope that you have" (1 Peter 3:15 NIV). The word translated "answer" is the Greek word *apologia*, which means "defense" or "reasoned reply." This "word was often used of the argument for the defense in a court of law," and it also referred to "an informal explanation or defense of one's position."[19] So the task of Christian apologetics involves providing a reasonable defense of the Christian faith, and every believer is called upon to be prepared to make such a defense when it is needed.

Now what Peter commands, Luke shows at work in his own writing and in the apostles' ministry. As New Testament scholar F. F. Bruce points out:

> Luke is...one of the first Christian
> apologists. In that particular type of
> apologetic which is addressed to the secular
> authorities to establish the law-abiding
> character of Christianity he is absolutely
> the pioneer. But other forms of apologetic
> appear in the course of his work, especially
> in some of the speeches of Acts. Thus,
> Stephen's speech in Ch. 7 is the prototype
> of Christian apologetic against the Jews,

designed to demonstrate that Christianity and not Judaism is the true fulfillment of the revelation given through Moses and the prophets. Similarly, Paul's speech at Athens in Ch. 17 is one of the earliest examples of Christian apologetic against the pagans, designed to show that the true knowledge of God is given in the gospel and not in the idolatrous vanities of paganism. And Paul's speech before Agrippa in Ch. 26 is, of course, the crowning *apologia* for his own missionary career.[20]

- *Have you ever heard a fellow Christian effectively present a case for the faith, whether through speaking, teaching, writing, or another form of media? If so, who was this person, and what was it about this person's presentation that affected you?*

- *Are you prepared to defend the Christian faith? If called upon, could you explain what you believe and why you believe it? Could you provide evidence that what Christianity teaches is true and trustworthy? Why or why not?*

 EXPERIENCE GOD'S HEART

History matters to God, which is why so much of the Bible contains books of history and why the writer of Hebrews appeals to believers from the past to encourage future generations of believers (Hebrews 11). Luke wrote his Luke-Acts volumes to give us a reliable, trustworthy history of Jesus and the first decades of the movement he spawned and guided. God works in history, revealing himself, his ways, and the path to peace and joy with him.

- *One way to experience God's heart is to learn about him through the books of history he has inspired in Scripture. The Bible books that focus on history are, in the Old Testament, Genesis through Esther and large segments of Daniel. In the New Testament, the books of history are the four Gospels and Acts. As you consider Bible books to study, be sure to include the history ones in the mix.*

- *Of course, God's work in history did not stop in the first century. To gain insight and understanding into his work through the church since then, add books on church history to your reading list. If you have never read one, we suggest starting with a one-volume work. Consult the information in the endnote for some recommended resources.[21]*

- *God's involvement in your life has a past too. Consider writing about his past work in your life, beginning with how you came to Christ and then moving on to your conversion and how God has been working to change you into the image of Christ through the power of the Spirit. Along the way, praise and thank him for his work in your life and ask him to fulfill his work in you and through you as you move ever closer to seeing him face-to-face and living in his presence forever.*

❤ SHARE GOD'S HEART

- *If you haven't already done this, develop the habit of bringing up your history of walking with Christ to family members, friends, work associates, and anyone else who needs to hear about the living God and his incredible activity in human lives over the centuries. You don't have to tell your whole life story in a single sitting. Instead, consider providing snapshots into your life with God, bringing them out naturally in conversation. This way people will begin to realize how vital your walk with God is and how it has shaped you into the person you are today. Through you, others may be drawn to Christ.*

Talking It Out

Since Christians grow in community, not just in solitude, every "Talking It Out" section contains questions you may want to discuss with another person or in a group. Here are the exercises for this lesson.

1. Read through Acts and take notes on what stands out to you. Then get together with some individuals who are studying Acts now or have studied it before. Share what you picked up on, and then have them do the same. Let this time orient you (and the rest of the group) to this early history of the Christian movement called the church.

---

2. Acts depicts the church's advances as well as some of the opposition it faced. When you look at the church today, where do you see the church making effective inroads into people's lives and their culture, and where do you see roadblocks put up to try to stop the church or hinder its growth?

Part 1

Messengers to Jerusalem

(1:2–6:7)

LESSON 2

Jesus Keeps His Promise

(1:2–2:47)

After Luke identifies his recipient and links Acts with his Gospel (Acts 1:1), he shares some facts about Jesus' last days on earth, some of which he had mentioned in his Gospel's last two chapters. But he also adds some information, especially about what Jesus told his disciples before he ascended into heaven.

Spirit-Filled Instructions

- *Luke makes it clear in his Gospel that the Holy Spirit empowered Jesus throughout his entire earthly life. Read the following passages from Luke's Gospel and write down what they reveal about the role the Spirit played at various times in Jesus' life. You may need to read some of the surrounding verses of each passage to gain perspective on their context.*

1:15–17

1:35

1:80

3:16

3:21–22

4:1–2

4:14–15

4:16–19

10:21

- *Now turn to Acts 1:2. Through whom and to whom did the resurrected Jesus give his final instructions? What does this tell you about the Spirit's role, even in Jesus' resurrection life?*

- *Luke tells us that Jesus verified that he had risen from the dead through "many convincing signs" (v. 3). He also summarizes these signs. What were they?*

- *Review the Gospel of Luke, chapter 24 and write out the specifics about Jesus' resurrection evidence that support the summary Luke provides in Acts 1:3.*

- *Luke records at least a summary of what Jesus instructed his disciples to do before he arose into heaven. Read the passages from Acts 1 listed below and summarize next to each one what Jesus told his disciples:*

     Verses 4–5:

     Verses 6–8:

Jesus promised his followers that the same powerful one who had empowered him and his ministry—namely, the Holy Spirit—would also empower them and their mission (v. 5). What Jesus promised them would also be for all who put their faith in him (Romans 8:1–17; 1 Corinthians 12; Galatians 5:16–26). The church is Spirit-powered because every believer receives the Spirit when they receive the Son by faith.

- *What would you say the Holy Spirit does in the lives of believers? Be as specific as you can.*

• *Have you seen the Spirit work in your life in any of those ways? If so, which ones?*

In Acts 1:6, the disciples showed that they still hoped that the coming of the Spirit would indicate the political liberation of Israel from Roman rule. But Jesus did not confirm this hope. Instead, he shifted the disciples' focus to what he wanted them to do, starting in Jerusalem and eventually extending "even to the remotest places on earth" (v. 8). And then what follows in Acts shows the disciples engaging in this mission through the power and guidance of the Spirit.

> Jesus' mandate to witness not only gives us the theme of Acts but also a basic table of contents by the threefold reference to "Jerusalem," "all Judea and Samaria," and "the ends of the earth." To be sure, Luke's development of the table of contents is fuller and more subtle than its succinct form here. Nevertheless, in what follows he shows through a series of vignettes how the mission of the church in its witness to Jesus fared at Jerusalem (2:42–8:3), throughout Judea and Samaria (8:4–12:24), and as it progressed until it finally reached the imperial capital city of Rome (12:25–28:31).[22]

Of course, this mission for Christ's followers to be his messengers, his witnesses, has been going on ever since the first disciples were initially empowered by the Holy Spirit (Acts 2). The church has been carrying out this mission for two thousand years, bringing the good news about Jesus Christ to every people group on the globe. This needs to keep occurring because new people are born and raised, and they need to hear the gospel (the good news) too.

- *Are you sharing with other people the good news about Jesus? If so, how? If not, why?*

Heavenly Ascension

- *After he had finished instructing his followers, Jesus ascended to heaven.[23] Summarize this event below (1:9–11).*

- *Why do you think it was important for Jesus to physically leave his disciples rather than remain with them? For help, see Luke 24:45–49; John 14:15–26; 16:4–11.*

- *Do you realize that although Jesus is not physically with us, he is spiritually present to all of us through his Spirit? That he is working through us and in us by the Holy Spirit? Does that encourage you? If so, in what way? If not, why?*

Replenishing the Twelve

- *Right after Jesus' ascension, what did his disciples do (Acts 1:12–14)?*

- *Along with eleven of the twelve original disciples, Luke mentions Jesus' family members (vv. 13–14). Who were these family members? Why was having his brothers there significant (see note 'h' associated with verses 13–14 for assistance)?*

- *How many believers were gathered together, and what did Peter tell them they needed to do and why (vv. 15–20)?*

- *What qualifications had to be met for a new apostle (vv. 21–22)?*

- *Which two candidates fit those qualifications, and how did the disciples make their final choice (vv. 23–26)?*

# WORD WEALTH

According to Proverbs 16:33, "The lot is cast into the lap, but its every decision is from the LORD" (NIV). In Scripture, casting lots was often used for making important decisions.

> Aaron, on the Day of Atonement, chose by lot one of the goats for a scapegoat to bear the sins of the people into the wilderness (Lev 17:7–10, 21, 22). The division of the land of [Palestine] after the conquest was accomplished by lot (Josh 14:2; 18:6; 1 Chron 6:54ff.). The service of the Temple, including the music (1 Chron 25:7, 8), the doorkeepers (26:13ff.), and the supply of wood fuel for the altar were regulated by casting lots (Neh 10:34ff.). The guilt of suspected criminals was established by lot (Josh 7:14; 1 Sam 14:42).[24]

Lots may have consisted of stones, wood, arrows, or animal bones. When the apostles decided to replace Judas, they may have written the names of Matthias and Barsabbas on stones, placed those stones "in a cloth bag or vessel, and then the first stone drawn out named the one selected."[25] With the apostles' lot casting bathed in prayer and a selection process that included clear and justifiable qualifications for the candidates and a scriptural rationale for replacing Judas, they expected that whoever the lot designated would be God's choice, and so it was. The Twelve were restored with the addition of Matthias.

Here Comes the Spirit!

The Spirit came to the one hundred twenty gathered disciples on "the day of Pentecost" in Jerusalem (Acts 2:1). Pentecost was a Jewish festival that came "fifty days after the first Sabbath after

Passover (Exod. 23:15–17; 34:22; Lev. 23:15–21; Num. 28:26; Deut. 16:9–12). It was also known as the 'Feast of Weeks' or 'Day of Firstfruits.'"[26] Bible scholar Harold Hoehner gives the date for this event as May 24, 33.[27]

- How did the Spirit's presence manifest itself to the gathered disciples (Acts 2:2–3)? Consult study note 'c' for verse 3.

- What did the Spirit's presence enable the disciples to do (v. 4)?

- Who else witnessed the event, and what amazed them about it (vv. 5–12)?

- *What was the counter-response by some doubters in the crowd (v. 13)?*

- *How would you assess the critics' claim? What evidence would you point to that would undermine their claim?*

Defense of the Spirit's Arrival

The apostle Peter stands up as a spokesman for the other eleven apostles and defends (offers an *apologia* for) the genuineness and truth of what the gathered crowd had witnessed.

- *Whom did Peter specifically address (2:14)?*

- *What was his direct challenge to the charge of drunkenness (v. 15)?*

- *What did Peter contend was the truth about what the crowds had witnessed (vv. 16–21)?*

Peter then turned his attention to the last line of Joel's prophecy, "Everyone who calls on the name of the Lord will be saved" (v. 21; see Joel 2:32). Who is this Lord? That was the matter Peter addressed.

- *What did Peter point to as the "facts" of the matter, and whom did they concern (Acts 2:22–24)?*

- *Peter then anchored his interpretation of these facts
  in a prophecy spoken by King David centuries before.
  Summarize this prophecy in your own words (vv. 25–28).*

- *What was Peter's interpretation and explanation of
  David's prophetic words (vv. 29–31)?*

- *Whom did Peter equate with the Messiah of David's
  prophecy, and how did he connect that to Joel's prophecy
  about the coming of the "promised Holy Spirit" (vv. 32–33)?*

- *Peter then cites another prophecy from David. What does he say about it, and what conclusion does he draw from it and the rest of what he has argued (vv. 34–36)?*

- *How effective was Peter's defense? How did the crowd respond (vv. 37–41)?*

- *After their repentance of sin, in whom were the penitent to be baptized? What gift would come along with that and why (vv. 38–39)?*

The Early Church Community

Luke provides a description of the early Jerusalem church as he closes out chapter 2 of Acts.

- *Read verses 42–47 and write down the characteristics, the traits, of the community of faith during this time period.*

- *What among these traits stands out to you the most and why?*

- *What was the Lord's response to this community of believers (v. 47)?*

EXPERIENCE GOD'S HEART

With Jesus comes the Spirit. Not only did Jesus promise to send him, but when we repent of our sins and ask Jesus to come into our life as our Savior and Lord, he comes, and with him comes the gift of the Holy Spirit.

- *If you already know Jesus by faith, you already have his Spirit in your life. Rely on that fact. Turn to Galatians 5:22–26 and meditate on the truths expressed there. What among the Spirit's fruit have you seen manifested in your life? It will not show up perfectly, but the Spirit's fruit will come through in your life the more you yield to him.*

SHARE GOD'S HEART

Peter wanted the Jews of his day to know the identity of the true Lord and Messiah, which he said was Jesus, the one who had been crucified and had risen alive from the dead. Jesus is the good news! God has come among us, walked and talked, healed and raised the dead, taught and illustrated the truths about God and his kingdom, taken our punishment on the cross, defeated death through his resurrection, and ascended into heaven, where he rules over all and awaits a day when he will return and establish his all-good and all-just rule on earth forever and ever. God will once again walk among his people. Everyone who calls upon Jesus will be saved and will be able to enjoy this incredible relationship with God forever.

- *When was the last time you shared this good news with others? It's God's heart "for everyone to embrace his life and return to the full knowledge of the truth" (1 Timothy 2:4). Begin praying for neighbors, friends, family members, work associates...anyone you know who needs to hear the good news about Jesus. If the list is too long, shorten it to a more manageable size or group the names into lists of five or fewer. If you group them, pray for one group one day and then another group on a different day and so on. Then, as you pray for these individuals, look for opportunities to tell them about Jesus, asking the Spirit to prepare the way.*

Talking It Out

1. Review the characteristics of the early church in Acts 2:42–47. Which of these traits does your local church, Bible study group, or other Christian relationships exhibit? How do you account for the presence of these characteristics? In other words, from what you can tell, do they seem to be indicators of God's presence and work in the relationships or community, or do they seem to be the result of mere human effort?

2. If any of the community traits revealed in the final verses of Acts 2 are not present in your Christian community or relationships, why do you think this is so? What, if anything, do you think you can do to help bring about those missing characteristics?

3. When Peter made his case for the true nature of the Spirit's presence and power among Jesus' followers, he provided reasons that Jews were more likely to accept. He argued from the writings of fellow Jews (Joel and David), and he built his case on an understanding of God and his works that were also grasped through the writings and national history of the Jews. If you were speaking to someone with a much different background, what might be some reasons for faith that you would provide that this person might more readily accept?

LESSON 3

Church Expansion and Threats

(3:1–6:7)

Jesus had told his disciples to wait for the Spirit in Jerusalem. They obeyed. Then the Spirit came, demonstrating his presence with fire and his power through language. He reversed the confusion of tongues that happened by divine judgment at Babel so long ago—a confusion that separated people groups from one another (Genesis 11:1–9).[28] Rather than creating confusion and division, the Spirit caused Jesus' disciples to speak in human languages they had never studied so that the people they spoke to would hear in their own languages what the disciples said. It must have been amazing to witness a united message voiced through multiple languages and heard and understood by all the different language speakers present.

After explaining the miracle and tying it to the fulfillment of prophecy and the person and work of Jesus Christ, the one hundred twenty disciples enlarged their ranks by three thousand (Acts 2:41). Then daily their numbers grew as the Lord kept working among them and through them (v. 47). The church in Jerusalem was growing and growing quickly. It was bound to catch the attention of the Jewish religious authorities, and it did.

The Power of His Name

All of Acts 3 tells about an event that occurred at the temple complex in Jerusalem. It was this event that provoked the ire of the religious officials there.

- *Who went up to the temple, and whom did they first encounter there (Acts 3:1–2)?*

- *What request did the man at the gate make, and how did the two apostles respond (vv. 2–6)?*

- *What happened to the unnamed man? How did he respond to this miraculous change, and what kind of attention did he draw (vv. 7–11)?*

- *Peter took the opportunity to speak to the assembled crowd. By what name did he address them? What did he ask them, and by what power and authority did he say the man experienced healing (vv. 12–16)?*

- *When Peter spoke about Jesus and the crowd of Jews before him, in what ways did he relate his audience to Jesus and Jesus to them (vv. 13–15)?*

- *Still speaking to the crowd, Peter expanded on points he had made already. Read verses 16–26 and summarize his main points.*

- *Peter's talk is a mixture of condemnation, hope, and blessing. For what did he condemn his fellow Jews? What blessing did he say had come upon them? What hope did they have as a result (vv. 13–26)?*

- *How many people came to faith in Christ as a result of what these apostles said and did (4:4)?*

- *What might you have concluded about God, his justice, and his grace and mercy if you had been standing in that crowd?*

Whose Power and Authority?

Their Arrest

Not everyone carefully considered what the apostles taught, and certainly not all accepted what the apostles said. Some people became infuriated, rejecting out of hand the apostles' teaching.

- *Who became incensed at Peter and John's words (4:1–2)? What did they do to stop these two apostles (v. 3)?*

 THE BACKSTORY

Luke mentions two groups and one individual who were upset with Peter and John.

The "captain of the temple police" (vv. 1–2) was the commanding officer of that enforcement group. "He was considered inferior in rank only to the high priest and had the responsibility of maintaining order in the temple precincts."[29] New Testament scholar Darrell Bock notes that this police captain was also "a member of the high-priestly family" and a Levite, as were many of the temple police. Along with keeping the peace, he was tasked with disallowing "any messianic expectations that Rome would dislike (John 11:47–48)."[30] The fact that the apostles were proclaiming that Jesus was the long-awaited Messiah would have greatly concerned this captain. Also, he may have been present at (or at least partly responsible for) Jesus' arrest in the garden of Gethsemane (Luke 22:52).

The "priests" (Acts 4:1–2) were "the officials responsible for the temple (particularly for the sacrifices, for other rituals at the Jewish festivals, and matters such as the temple tax)."[31] Some of them had also been part of the party who had arrested Jesus (Luke 22:52).

The Sadducees (Acts 4:1–2) were "members of the priestly families" who formed part of the aristocracy in Jerusalem.[32] They were a significant, though minority, Jewish sect that denied the resurrection and accepted only the Torah (the first five books of the Old Testament) as divinely inspired. Of course, the apostles relied on Scriptures that went beyond the Torah, and they preached that Jesus had risen from the dead. The apostles had also proclaimed that Jesus was the Messiah, another claim that the Sadducees rejected. For this sect, "the Messiah was an ideal, not a person, and the Messianic Age was a process, not a cataclysmic or even datable event. Furthermore, as political rulers and dominant landlords...they stressed cooperation with Rome and maintenance of the status quo."[33] Most of the priests belonged to this sect, and the captain of the temple guard was always a Sadducee, as were each of the high priests.[34]

As you can see, the apostles had the deck stacked against them once they began publicly proclaiming Jesus, his resurrection, and his messiahship within the confines of the temple courts.

The Hearing

The next day following their arrest, the apostles Peter and John were brought before a gathering of Jewish religious leaders in Jerusalem for questioning (Acts 4:5).

- *Which groups and individuals were there (vv. 5–6)?*

THE BACKSTORY

This collection of groups and individuals were members of the Sanhedrin. The Sanhedrin was a "seventy-one-member tribunal that served as the Jewish supreme court."[35] It exercised "jurisdiction in all noncapital cases—though it also advised the Roman governors in capital cases." The Sanhedrin could impose the death penalty upon gentiles who trespassed "beyond the posted barriers into the inner courts of the temple." This Jewish ruling body "consisted of the high priest, who by virtue of his office was president, and seventy others, made up of members of the high priestly families, a few influential persons of various formal ideological allegiances or backgrounds within Judaism, and professional experts in the law drawn from both Sadducean and Pharisaic ranks."[36] The dominant party of the Sanhedrin was the Sadducees.

Luke provides the names of some of the individuals who were among the Sanhedrin when Peter and John appeared before them. One was "Annas the high priest" (v. 6). He had served as high priest from AD 615, so at this particular hearing, he had not been the high priest for many years. The fact that he is called high priest "underscores his standing in the Sanhedrin."[37] He was still a highly respected and influential figure. And it was before Annas that Jesus had been interrogated on the evening of his arrest (John 18:13, 19–24).

Luke also mentions the presence of Caiaphas (Acts 4:6). He was Annas' son-in-law, and he had been the high priest during Jesus' trial and had led the Sanhedrin to declare Jesus guilty of blasphemy (John 18:13, 19–24; see also Matthew 26:57–66). He was still the high priest when Peter and John came before the Sanhedrin in the year 33. He served as high priest from AD 18–36.

As for John and Alexander, two other members of the Sanhedrin that Luke mentions, we have no other certain information about them. It's possible that "John was the son of Caiaphas, who would one day be the high priest." It might also be the case that John and Alexander were "leaders of the Sadducees."[38]

So two of Jesus' followers—in fact, two of the original Twelve—now stood before the same Jewish tribunal with many of the same religious leaders who had falsely charged Jesus, condemned him to death, and urged the Roman governor Pilate to execute him.

- *What did the Sanhedrin ask the apostles John and Peter (Acts 4:7)? To what were the religious leaders referring when they mentioned "these things"? See chapter 3 of Acts and the opening verses of chapter 4 for help.*

- *Who was the spokesman for the two apostles, and who empowered his response (v. 8)?*

- *Read verses 8–12 and summarize the defense that Peter made and its tone.*

- *After reading what Peter said, whom would you say was really on trial—the apostles or the Sanhedrin? Explain your answer.*

- *What was the response of the Sanhedrin after Peter's speech (vv. 13–18)?*

- *Did the apostles intend to comply with the order from the Sanhedrin? On what basis did the apostles justify their response (vv. 19–20)?*

- *How did the public respond to what happened (vv. 21–22)?*

❤ SHARE GOD'S HEART

At least two truths stand out in this part of Acts: (1) Salvation is through Jesus alone (v. 12), and (2) we must obey God over man (vv. 19–20). Both truths point to the primacy and supremacy of God and his will over man and man's will. God is first. Period. When his revealed will comes into conflict with that of any of his creatures, no matter the position they hold, they must adhere to what God commands. His authority is paramount.

Perhaps the most important way we can share God's heart is to obey him first and foremost. He has declared that salvation comes through his Son, Jesus Christ, and not through anyone else. Therefore, when we share the good news of salvation with others, we dare not shrink back from declaring this truth. Jesus is the one and only Savior. Everlasting life is found in him and in him alone.

And when it comes to obeying a human dictate that contradicts, undermines, or seeks to supersede the clear command of God, we must obey God, not human law.

- *When you share the faith with others, do you put Christ front and center? Do you make it clear that salvation is in Jesus alone? Why or why not?*

- *Why does it matter that we tell others that Jesus is the only Savior?*

• *Have you ever faced a conflict between what a human authority demanded that you do and what God commanded you to do? How did you respond? Would you respond differently given what you now know? If so, what would your response look like?*

• *What can your courage to stand up for God's way potentially do for those who witness your stand?*

Power and Proclamation Spread

After John and Peter were released from custody, they "went to the other believers and explained all that had happened" (Acts 4:23).

• *How did these believers respond to the apostles' report (vv. 24–30)?*

- *What happened in response to the prayer of these believers (v. 31)?*

- *Notice how God blessed the apostles' obedience in continuing to speak courageously about Jesus rather than complying with the Sanhedrin's command "to never teach the people or speak again using the name of Jesus" (v. 18). How do you imagine the Sanhedrin responded to their disobedience? How do governing authorities typically treat people who violate their dictates?*

The Church, Judgment, and Healing

A Generous Community

Once again, Luke provides insight into the Jerusalem church, including the character and key activities of its members.

- *Read verses 32–37.*

  Which traits revealed in these verses show the character of the early Christians?

  Which of their activities did Luke choose to highlight?

  What was a benefit of their character and activities that impacted the entire faith community?

Costly Deceit

No community is perfect, not even a Christian one. All human beings are fallen, and even Christians still struggle with their fallen natures (see, for example, Romans 7:15–25). Sometimes, however, our sin can exact a severe price.

- *Read Acts 5:1–2. What did the married couple, Ananias and Sapphira, choose to do?*

- *When the husband, Ananias, brought to the apostles a portion of their earnings from selling their farm, what did God reveal to Peter (v. 3)?*

- *What truths did Peter's statements and questions to Ananias reveal about this couple's actions (vv. 3–4)?*

- *What happened to Ananias (vv. 5–6)?*

- *Three hours later, Sapphira, Ananias' wife, came before the apostles, and she had no idea what had happened to her husband (v. 7). What did Peter ask her, and what does Sapphira's answer reveal about her partnership with her husband regarding the proceeds from selling their land (v. 8)?*

- *What did Peter then tell her, and what happened to Sapphira as a result (vv. 9–10)?*

- *How did the entire church in Jerusalem respond to the news of this couple's deceit and demise (v. 11)?*

Luke notes that what Ananias and Sapphira did also involved a confrontation between Satan and the Holy Spirit. Ananias had allowed Satan to motivate him to act deceptively and to conspire with his wife to carry out the deception in a way that would make them appear far more generous before fellow Christians than they actually were. This couple was not under compulsion to turn over all that they had earned from selling their land (v. 4). They could have used the funds as they saw fit. Instead, they pretended "that they were contributing all the proceeds while in reality retaining some for themselves."[39] Human praise was far more important to them than integrity and honesty, and this led them to lie to God and serve Satan.

The biblical text doesn't say that God struck each spouse dead. And yet, it's clear from the church's response to their deaths that the "fear of God" rose to new heights, thus associating their deaths with divine judgment. As New Testament scholar Eckhard Schnabel explains:

> Peter does not utter a word of judgment,
> nor do his words condemn Ananias to death,
> nor does he express a wish that he would
> die. However, as the apostle has just blamed
> Ananias for lying against God (v. 4), and as
> he has unmasked Ananias's heart as being
> driven by Satan (v. 3), his sudden death
> must be understood as God's judgment.
> As Peter laid bare Ananias's heart and
> stated his rebellion against God, Ananias's
> heart gives out. Whether he dies of a heart
> attack, induced by the public exposure
> of his deceit in front of the apostles and
> perhaps in front of thousands of believers in
> Solomon's Portico, or whether his death has
> supernatural causes, its timing certainly is
> the result of divine judgment.[40]

The same can be said of the death of Sapphira. The apostles and the rest of the church saw in their deaths the judgment of God. The fear of God that arose among the congregation of believers involved "the distressing apprehension that God has intervened in judgment, the alarming realization that he may do so again in other cases of deception, and the terrifying trepidation that one's own life might be in jeopardy because of sins that one has committed."[41]

♥ EXPERIENCE GOD'S HEART

The writer of Hebrews tells us: "Since we are receiving our rights to an unshakable kingdom we should be extremely thankful and offer God the purest worship that delights his heart as we lay down our lives in absolute surrender, filled with awe. For our God is a holy, devouring fire" (Hebrews 12:28–29). Ananias and Sapphira conspired to deceive in order to exalt themselves. Rather than surrender themselves to God, they lied to him. Rather than bow before him, they gave in to Satan. Rather than act according to God's will, they tested him. It's true that God is gracious, merciful, and kind. But he is also a "devouring fire." He deserves our "absolute surrender," our "awe," our thankfulness, our everything.

- *Have you surrendered your all to God? If not, why? What is holding you back?*

- *If you have given God your all, are you making decisions that fit with that level of commitment to him? If not, why?*

Surrendering to God is not a once-for-all-time act. We need to do it daily, sometimes often during the day. He wants to give us so much! He saves us to bless us. His blessings are pouring out much like the rushing water of Niagara Falls. If we hold our buckets (our heart, mind, and will) upright, they will fill to over-flowing! But if we choose to disobey and thereby turn our buckets sideways or even upside down, the flowing blessings may dribble in somewhat or even bypass us. The choice is ours.

Growth and Healing

Once again, Luke turns to describe the state of the early church. Despite some sin that had appeared in its ranks, the church was still showing incredible signs of God's work in it and through it. According to Hoehner, the year was likely 34 or 35.[42]

- *Read Acts 5:12–16. What does Luke reveal about the leaders of the early church? About the believers they led?*

- *In those same verses, what does Luke report about the effectiveness of the early church's ministry?*

- *What was the church's reputation among the people in Jerusalem and surrounding areas?*

A Failed Persecution

Recall that the Sanhedrin had told Peter and John "to never teach the people or speak again using the name of Jesus" (4:18). Rather than obey this governing Jewish body, the apostles said they would obey God over these human rulers (v. 19). And this is what they did—over and over again. Consequently, thousands more individuals came to Christ as their Savior, countless people were healed, more miracles occurred, and Christians were increasingly "held...in high regard" (5:13). The growth and vitality of the church seemed unstoppable.

- *How did the leading Jewish religious officials respond to all of this and why (5:17–18)?*

- *How did God and his apostles respond (vv. 19–25)? Explain how this surprised and frustrated the Jewish religious leaders.*

- *After the apostles were rearrested, summarize the exchange that occurred between them and the Sanhedrin ("the council"; vv. 26–32).*

- *How did the Sanhedrin deal with the apostles' bold stand (vv. 33–40)?*

- *Did the Sanhedrin's actions deter the apostles or inspire them (vv. 41–42)? Explain your answer.*

 THE BACKSTORY

Gamaliel gave two examples of men who started new movements that came to nothing. Theudas was one of these individuals, and despite gaining a following of about four hundred men, "he was killed" and "all of his followers were scattered" (v. 36). Outside of the New Testament, we know nothing else with certainty of Theudas and his claims and movement.[43]

The second person is a different story. Judas the Galilean led a revolt, and the Jewish historian Flavius Josephus wrote about it almost ninety years after it occurred. While the end of this Judas was similar to that of Theudas, what Judas began led to more revolts, which culminated in a war against the Roman Empire that started in AD 66, led to the destruction of Jerusalem and its temple in 70, and ended with the fall of the rebels at Masada in 73. In the year 6, Judas "inaugurated a religious and nationalist revolt, contending that God alone was Israel's true King, and that it was, therefore, high treason against God to pay tribute to Caesar." While the revolt was crushed by Rome, "the movement lived on in the party of the Zealots."[44] Historian Corey Piper describes this Judas-led revolt and the Roman census that precipitated it as having the significance in Jewish history equivalent to "Japan's attack on Pearl Harbor in 1941 or the terrorist airplane attacks on US targets on September 11, 2001. A subversive war started that lasted for another 70 years. Josephus wrote extensively about the horrors that came upon the Jews during this time in his account *The Wars of the Jews*, which culminated with the destruction of the temple in Jerusalem. He traced the entire tragedy back to these Zealots and this revolt led by Judas of Galilee."[45]

Added Leaders

The more the church grew, the more needs and complaints arose within its ranks. Luke tells about one of these matters that led to the addition of leaders who were called upon to assist the apostles in an important ministry.

• Read Acts 6:1–7, and then answer the following questions:

What was the situation that arose that required attention (v. 1; see also the study notes 'b' and 'c' for this verse)?

What did the apostles propose for a solution (vv. 2–4)?

How did the members of the church receive their proposal, and what was the result (vv. 5–7)?

• Are your church leaders responsive to needs that arise within the congregation? Are you willing to serve to help meet any of these needs? Prayerfully consider if you are equipped to be a servant-leader in your church. If so, ask God to help you be open to how you can assist your church's leaders in ministry and be available when the need arises. If you don't see yourself in such a role, ask God to enable you to spot others in the congregation who may be able to serve where a need exists. All of us are not called to be leaders, but all of us are called to serve others in some capacity.

Talking It Out

1. To say that Jesus is the only one "to whom God has given authority by which we must experience salvation" (Acts 4:12) may seem shocking, intolerant, and exclusive. But is it? All truth is exclusive. If it is true that you live alone, then that excludes many billions of people who do not live with you. If you live in, say, Phoenix, Arizona, that excludes every other place on earth and in the entire universe. Is it really tolerant to say that you are someone else or that you live somewhere else—or is it simply false? Discuss this matter, relating it back to Jesus as the only way to salvation. If he is—and Scripture says he is—then does denying this or broadening this in some way improve the claim, or does it actually falsify it?

2. The apostles and fellow believers in Jesus Christ stood their ground against opposition, even when that opposition came from governing authorities. Discuss how and why they did this and what we can learn from them if and when we face opposition too.

3. Acts does not present silent believers. Early Christians were vocal about what they believed and why they believed it. Luke gives no indication that they were obnoxious, but they did speak up. In fact, they refused to be silenced. Do you have the courage of your Christian convictions? Are you willing to speak up and not remain silent? How can you share your faith in the contexts in which you live: at home, in your neighborhood, at work, at church, at entertainment events, etc.? Talk about various ways you can speak and demonstrate the truth about what you believe and why.

Part 2

Messengers to All Judea and Samaria

(6:8–9:31)

LESSON 4

The Ministry and Martyrdom of Stephen

(6:8–8:3)

Jesus was arrested, tried, and crucified under false charges. He went to his death an innocent man. Before all of this happened to him, he warned his followers:

> Be on your guard! For there will be those who will betray you before their religious councils and brutally beat you with whips in their public gatherings. And because you follow me, they will take you to stand trial in front of rulers and even kings as an opportunity to testify of me before them and the unbelievers. So when they arrest you, don't worry about how to speak or what you are to say, for the Holy Spirit will give you at that very moment the words to speak. (Matthew 10:17–19)

Jesus knew that his disciples would face persecution for their trust in him. The students of Jesus would not get better treatment than Jesus himself did.

And so it was—and still is. The Jewish authorities arrested

Peter and John and commanded them to stop teaching about Jesus or even using his name (Acts 4:18). But Peter and John refused to comply, as did the rest of the apostles and Christ-followers. Later, the council arrested all the apostles, severely beat them, and commanded them also not to speak anymore in the name of Jesus (5:40). The apostles also refused to obey the religious authorities. Instead, "they kept preaching every day in the temple courts and went from house to house, preaching the gospel of Jesus" (v. 42).

So far in Acts, the apostles endured persecution, but no one had their life taken. They and their fellow Christians kept spreading the gospel despite the demands of the religious authorities.

This was soon to take an ugly turn.

Stephen, the Man

Stephen, one of the church's chosen servant leaders, became the tipping point toward a more aggressive and deadly persecution of the church.

- *What was Stephen appointed to do to help the apostles (Acts 6:2–6)?*

- *How does Luke describe Stephen (vv. 5, 8)?*

- *Along with the service ministry Stephen engaged in, what else did he do (vv. 8–10)?*

The Set-up

Stephen's ministry "upset some men belonging to a sect who called themselves the Men Set Free" (v. 9). These men were nationalistically diverse: Libyans, Egyptians, and Turks (v. 9). And they were part of one or more synagogues in Jerusalem. According to New Testament scholar Eckhard J. Schnabel:

> A synagogue…was a meeting place for Jews to discuss community issues, share meals, adjudicate infractions of the [Mosaic] law and of [Jewish] tradition, collect and distribute charitable funds for purposes of social welfare, provide elementary education, study Torah, and store the scrolls of the Holy Scriptures and other material; it was also a place of residence for synagogue officials and a hostel for visiting Jews. Not all synagogues had all these functions, but synagogues did not exclusively focus on "worship services" with prayers, readings from the Torah and from the Prophets, and sermons; they also dealt with communal affairs.[46]

While diverse in some ways, these Jewish men were united in their antagonism toward Stephen's message (v. 9). Luke doesn't specify exactly what Stephen said or did that agitated these men. Luke does, however, tell us who had the upper hand in the exchange and why and what that momentum led to.

- *How did Stephen fare in his exchange with the Men Set Free (vv. 9–10)?*

- *Since these Jewish men could not refute Stephen's arguments, what did they do in an attempt to silence him (vv. 11–12)?*

- *What were the specific accusations against Stephen (vv. 13–14)?*

- *With the case laid out against Stephen, what did the Sanhedrin ("the supreme council," v. 12) do? How did Stephen appear to them, and what question did the high priest finally ask him (6:15–7:1)?*

Stephen's Defense

Stephen appeared unruffled by the false charges laid out against him. His face even glowed like that of an angel! Undaunted and having already demonstrated "remarkable wisdom" and an irrefutable case (6:10), Stephen was fully prepared to address the accusations. His defense is the longest speech in Acts. And it is not just a defense, simply countering the charges against him. Stephen also "goes on the offensive, employing the strategy of *refutation*, which involves 'an overturning of something that has been proposed.'"[47] Recall the charges against Stephen: (1) he denigrated the Jewish temple; (2) he denigrated Jewish law; and (3) he claimed that Jesus would destroy the temple and change the traditions and customs that came down from Moses (vv. 13–14). In his refutation, Stephen set out to challenge each charge by drawing from the biblical story of the Jews as laid out in their Scriptures (the Old Testament) before he arrived at Jesus as the fulfillment of the Jewish prophetic pronouncements. Throughout, he pointed out an irrefutable proof: it was his accusers—his fellow Jews—who had a proven track record of disobeying the very God and his revelation that they so tenaciously claimed to uphold. In reality, they were the ones on trial, not Stephen.

From Abraham to Joseph

Stephen started with the father of Israel, Abraham.

- *Whom did Stephen address, and what does that tell you about how Stephen saw himself in relationship to his audience, the Sanhedrin (7:2)?*

- *Whom did God reveal himself to, and what did God tell him to do (vv. 2–4)? Did this individual obey God?*

- *Although Abraham moved all the way to the promised land, what did God give him instead of his own parcel of land (vv. 5–8)?*

- *Did Abraham carry out his side of the covenant during his lifetime? How do you know (v. 8)?*

- *Which descendants of Abraham did Stephen then mention, and what did they do (vv. 9–14)?*

- *Did Joseph's brothers bless and protect him even though he was a child of the covenant, just as they were? Why did the brothers behave this way, and who intervened to eventually rescue the covenant people from disaster?*

• *What indication did Stephen give to show that the covenant people believed in God's promise to give them their own land (vv. 15–16)?*

Moses and the Law

So far in his presentation of the history of God's chosen people, Stephen has highlighted their obedience, with the exception of Joseph's brothers. Still, what Joseph's brothers did could have led to disaster for the chosen line if God had not stepped in through the very brother they had attempted to get rid of forever. Then Stephen moves to Moses, the exodus, and the law. Here the obstinacy and unbelief of the covenant people increases dramatically.

• *When did God decide was the time to fulfill his land promise to Abraham (v. 17)?*

• *God's chosen people were facing opposition. Who was against them, and what did he do to them (vv. 18–19)?*

- *Whom did Stephen bring up next (vv. 20–22)? How did God ensure that this man was saved and prepared to become a leader?*

- *What plan did Moses enact, and how well did it play out (vv. 23–29)? Who rejected Moses as leader?*

- *About how old was Moses when God appeared to him, and where was Moses living (vv. 23, 29–30)?*

- *How did Moses respond to God's self-revelation? What did God commission him to do (vv. 31–34)?*

- *Did Moses obey God? Whom did he lead out of Egypt (pay special attention to how Stephen describes them)? How did God show that he was with Moses (vv. 35–36)?*

- *Whom did Moses prophesy would one day come, and how did he want the people to respond to this person (v. 37)?*

- *After Moses received the law from God, how did his chosen people respond (vv. 38–41)?*

- *What punishment did God finally bring on the Israelites for their continued unfaithfulness to him (vv. 42–43)?*

A pattern was emerging. Stephen showed that God kept his side of the covenant. And leaders such as Abraham, Joseph, Moses, Joshua, and David did as well. However, the people they led failed over and over again. They "refused to obey" (v. 39), made idols and worshiped them, and offered animal sacrifices to false gods. The Israelites were repeatedly unfaithful even though God had given them worthy leaders and continually demonstrated his faithfulness to his word.

The Tabernacle and the Temple

What about the temple? Maybe its construction and presence presented a better side of his chosen people. The temple's predecessor was the tabernacle, which was built while the Israelites were in the wilderness, outside of the promised land. Stephen next turned his attention to it.

- *Through Moses, God revealed "the pattern of the tabernacle" (v. 44). Did Moses build it according to God's specifications?*

- *What was the history of the tabernacle after the wilderness wanderings (vv. 45–46)?*

God had the Israelites construct the tabernacle to provide a place of worship, a focus of his presence among them (Exodus 25:8–9). This divinely ordained structure could be dismantled and put back together, and it lasted into the reign of King David. David, then, wanted to build a permanent "dwelling place for the God of Jacob" (Acts 7:46), but God denied him that privilege (2 Samuel 7). Instead, God said that he would build a house for David—namely, a royal lineage that would last forever (vv. 8–13). In other words, while the tabernacle served to focus God's people in worship, it was temporary. God's way was to show himself present through much more than a structure.

- *Then Stephen turned to Solomon and the magnificent temple he built for God (Acts 7:47). But did that structure actually house the Creator (vv. 48–50)? Why not?*

The Jewish leaders, especially those who were in charge of the temple in Jerusalem, had placed far too much importance on that building. The God of the universe, "the Most High God" (v. 48), could not be housed by anything in his creation. He was over all things. Nothing he made or anything a human being made could ever contain him. He could not be managed by humanity, not even by his own people. The temple was fine and beautiful and serviceable for worship, but it was still just a human construction, and it did not confine God.

To reaffirm this truth, Stephen quoted Isaiah 66:1 in Acts 7:49. On the heels of Isaiah's words came verse 2: "There is one my eyes are drawn to: the humble one, the tender one, the trembling one who lives in awe of all I say." Stephen's audience would have known these words. They confirm that the Lord's true temple, where he may always be found, is with the humble, the tender-hearted, the ones who tremble before him and his Word. God dwells "with the bruised and lowly in spirit, those who are humble and quick to repent…those who are broken over their sin" (Isaiah 57:15; cf. Matthew 5:3). The transcendent, sovereign Lord who had delivered his people over and over again blessed them *not* because of their ethnicity, nationality, or worthiness. He blessed them because he had promised he would and in response to their soft hearts toward him. But the history of the Israelites showed that they had characteristically responded to him with hardened hearts.

The Indictment

Finally, Stephen laid out his concluding indictment against his accusers.

- *What does he charge them with (Acts 7:51–53)?*

- *Who is the "Righteous One" Stephen mentions (v. 52)?*

- *Now take each charge that the council had leveled against Stephen and offer your assessment of whether each charge was true:*

    Charge 1: Stephen denigrated the Jewish temple. Did he?

    Charge 2: Stephen denigrated the Jewish law that came down from Moses. Did he?

    Charge 3: Stephen claimed that Jesus would destroy the temple and change the traditions and customs that came down from Moses. Did he?

Mob Violence and Forgiveness

Stephen's portrayal of Israel's history and indictment of her people and leaders led to a visceral reaction. The Sanhedrin became unhinged.

- *What does Luke say about the Sanhedrin's reaction (v. 54)?*

• *What happened with Stephen? Where did his focus go (vv. 55–56)?*

• *What, then, did Stephen's accusers do in reaction to Stephen's vision of the exalted Christ, the Son of Man (vv. 57–59)?*

• *What did Stephen pray as the members of the Sanhedrin pelted him with stones (vv. 59–60)?*

• *Who witnessed and supported Stephen's violent execution (v. 58; 8:1)?*

• *After Stephen's death,[48] what took place (8:1–3)?*

❧ EXPERIENCE GOD'S HEART

In Jesus' famous sermon on the mount, he said: "How enriched you are when persecuted for doing what is right! For then you experience the realm of heaven's kingdom. How blessed you are when people insult and persecute you and speak all kinds of cruel lies about you because of your love for me! So leap for joy—since your heavenly reward is great. For you are being rejected the same way the prophets were before you" (Matthew 5:10–12). Suffering is painful, but suffering for doing what is right is good. And suffering because we stand up for Jesus and the truth about him puts us in the company of the great prophets and leaders who showed great courage and conviction even amid intense persecution. We may pay a steep price here in this fallen world, but God will honor us and reward us in his everlasting kingdom.

- *Is your practice of the faith clear enough for people to know you belong to Christ? If so, how is that going for you? Have you been picked on, teased, criticized, put down, or harassed because of your faith in Christ? What reactions have you faced?*

- *Are the accusations against you justified, or like those that were leveled against Stephen, are they false, perhaps even malicious? How have you responded to the accusations?*

♥ SHARE GOD'S HEART

Jesus received Stephen into his presence as stones pulverized him. With Jesus in his sights, Stephen called on him to forgive those who were murdering him. Stephen loved his enemies and blessed those who cursed him, just as his Lord had taught (Matthew 5:44).

- *How do you relate to your enemies—those who oppose you, continually criticize you, or wish or work for your downfall? Remember, one way Stephen loved those who falsely charged him was to go on the offensive and tell the truth about them. In the process, he also refuted their charges. Love speaks the truth, even to your enemies, even to those who seek to persecute you and falsely charge you. So how do you show love to your enemies?*

- *Stephen prayed for his accusers. Do you? If so, of what do your prayers consist? If not, start praying for them now. Your accusers may not change because of your prayers, but you will. Even how you behave toward them will change as you hold them before God in prayer.*

Talking It Out

1. Following Christ carries a cost. Sometimes people will be drawn to us and want to learn more about the One we follow and imitate. Sometimes people will believe we are strange, out of date, and even duped by what we believe and whom we have our faith in. Other times people will hate us—despise us, malign us, and mistreat us. What cost have you seen believers pay for their dedication to Christ? How do you explain the different reactions people have to Jesus-followers?

2. Are you aware of how Christians are sometimes treated in other countries? Take some time to go online and research what Christians face elsewhere in the world, then get together with some fellow Christians to share your findings. Pray for your brothers and sisters in Christ and pray for those who persecute them.

LESSON 5

From Philip to Saul

(8:4–9:31)

The gospel of Jesus Christ spread wherever his followers went. And sometimes persecution pushed them from one place to another, but it failed to stop them from telling others about Jesus, who he was, what he taught, how he lived, and why he died and rose alive from the grave.

In the first seven chapters of Acts, Luke tells about the growth and impact of the Christian movement in Jerusalem, the very center of Judaism. Even there, many people who had come to live or visit from distant lands witnessed the coming of the Holy Spirit in power and heard about Jesus, the long-awaited and prophesied Messiah. No doubt they sent news to relatives and friends outside of Jerusalem about what they had seen and heard and even, for many of them, embraced. The gospel had already shown itself to be bound neither ethnically nor nationally. But the disciples had followed the instructions of their Lord. They went to Jerusalem after his ascension and waited for the Holy Spirit to come. And they had his other words in mind as well—that they would be his "messengers to Jerusalem, throughout Judea, the distant provinces—even to the remotest places on earth" (Acts 1:8). While they had not physically ventured much outside of Jerusalem, persecution was now pushing many disciples to leave the city and the locales closest to it and venture into neighboring Samaria and even beyond. Luke says that wherever these believers went, "they preached the wonderful news of the word of God" (8:4). So even in the face of persecution, the good news continued to spread.

Philip in Samaria

Luke focuses on one of these believers, a man named Philip. He is likely the same Philip mentioned as one of "seven godly men" chosen to assist the apostles (6:2–5).

- *Where did Philip travel to, and what activities did he engage in (8:5–7)? (For a visual of Philip's journey, see the map in TPT titled "The Missions of Philip and Peter.")*

- *What was the overall response to Philip's ministry there (v. 8)?*

 # THE BACKSTORY

The area called Samaria was just north of Judea (the geographical region that included Jerusalem, Bethlehem, and Masada) and south of Galilee (a region that included places such as Nazareth, Capernaum, and Chorazin). Samaria was also west of the Jordan River. The people who lived there were called Samaritans. They saw themselves "as pure Israelites, the authentic heirs of the religion of Abraham and the patriarchs."[49] The Samaritans also rejected all the Old Testament except for the Torah (Genesis through Deuteronomy).

First-century Jews, however, "considered the Samaritans to be a half-breed race, descendants of foreign colonists who had intermarried with the Israelites of the northern kingdom after the Assyrian conquest" around 722 BC.[50] Jews publicly cursed them in their synagogues and refused to accept Samaritans as witnesses in Jewish courts. While Samaritans claimed to be of Jewish descent, the Jews refused to accept their claim. Moreover, while the center of Jewish worship was Jerusalem, for Samaritans it was Shechem, which was in northeast Samaria.[51]

Philip, a Jew, went into enemy territory, at least as Jews thought of Samaria in the first century. Showing love to his enemies, he brought to the Samaritans the gospel and its power to heal illnesses, cure the lame and paralyzed, and cast out demons. This demonstrated that Jesus was the Messiah, not just for the Jews, but also for the Samaritans.

- *Have you ever shared your faith with someone you disliked, perhaps even intensely disliked? If so, what happened?*

- *Consider making a list of two or three individuals whom you do not get along with. Bring them before the Lord in prayer, even daily. Ask him to open their hearts to him, to provide them with opportunities to hear and respond to the good news about Jesus. Remain open to the possibility that you may be one person God may use to present the gospel. He may not call on you to do this, but he can still work through your prayers to soften you to those whom you may despise but whom he still loves.*

Philip and Simon

While in Samaria, Philip sparked the interest of a local fascination, a man who had become a celebrity of sorts.

• *Read Acts 8:9–11 and write down what you learn about this man whose name was Simon.*

• *How did Simon the sorcerer respond to Philip and his ministry when he encountered it (vv. 12–13)?*

• *What led the apostles Peter and John to Samaria, and what did they do there (vv. 14–17)?*

- *What, then, did Simon desire from the apostles, and what was he willing to do for it (vv. 18–19)?*

- *How did Peter respond to Simon (vv. 20–23)?*

- *What did Simon do after Peter's rebuke (v. 24)?*

- *The biblical text does not tell us whether Simon repented of his sins. Why do you think Luke left this matter unresolved?*

- *In verse 25, Luke wraps up his comments about the Christian mission in Samaria. What does he say happened?*

DIGGING DEEPER

Scripture does not mention Simon the magician again. And even though Luke says that Simon "believed and was baptized" (v. 13), Peter's rebuke of Simon, including describing him as still being filled with "wickedness" and a man with "treachery" in his heart and "poisoned" with "jealous envy" (vv. 22–23), has led many Bible commentators to doubt the authenticity of Simon's Christian conversion. Furthermore, one of the earliest church fathers, Justin Martyr (ca. AD 100–165), who himself was a Samaritan Christian, said Simon "did mighty acts of magic, by virtue of the art of the devils operating in him." The Romans regarded Simon as "a god," and they honored him "with a statue" with an inscription that said, "To Simon the holy God."[52]

Close to Justin Martyr's time, the church father Irenaeus (ca. 130–ca. 200) published his multi-volume book *Against Heresies*. In it, he indicated that Simon did not follow the apostle Peter's admonition. Instead, Simon "set himself eagerly to contend against the apostles, in order that he himself might seem to be a wonderful being, and applied himself with still greater zeal to the study of the whole magic art, that he might the better bewilder and overpower multitudes of men."[53]

After Justin Martyr and Irenaeus, every church father who mentions Simon confirms and expands upon their account of Simon's life.

- *Luke affirms that Simon made a profession of faith in Jesus, and yet later accounts of Simon's life do not portray him as living a life consistent with his confession of faith. In fact, they talk about him as the origin of many heresies, beginning with the ones he initially spawned. How do you account for these reports of Simon's post-conversion life? Explain your answer.*

9 SHARE GOD'S HEART

- *Do you know anyone who, like Simon, has shown fear over divine judgment but has not taken the next step to get right with God? If so, what, if anything, are you doing to show this person the next step they should take? Are you also praying for him or her? Why or why not?*

We do not know all that is in anyone's heart, and we often don't see all that our words and actions for Christ accomplish. We are not called to be messengers of Jesus based on what results we see or don't see. Instead, all of us are called to participate in spreading the gospel and making disciples for Jesus. We may plant seeds and even water them, but it is God who brings life and growth (1 Corinthians 3:6–7). We need to be faithful to do our part and then leave the rest to God.

- *How are you faithful in evangelism (sharing the faith) and discipleship (teaching the faith)? If you are not active in either activity, what can you do to get started?*

Philip and an Ethiopian

Luke has not finished with Philip's role in the spread of the gospel. While still in Samaria, "the Lord's angel" directed Philip to travel south of Jerusalem and get on the "desert road to Gaza" (v. 26). This road was in a desolate area, and it was "the last water stop in southwestern Israel before entering the desert on the way to Egypt."[54] Philip obeyed the angel's command (v. 27).

- *Whom did Philip encounter on this road, and what was this person doing (vv. 27–28)?*

Ethiopia was south of Egypt, so this traveler was far from his homeland, and he was likely black as were his fellow Ethiopians. As the minister of finance for the queen of Ethiopia, he was one of the country's top officials. And the "chariot" he traveled in was a carriage designed for this use. The tense of the verb used for "reading" indicates that this official had been "reading over an extended period of time. Since he had probably bought the scroll he was reading in Jerusalem, he would have presumably started reading from the beginning" of the book of Isaiah. "By the time he met Philip, he had progressed to the section we call Isaiah 53."[55]

- *Read Acts 8:29–38. Summarize what occurred between Philip and the Ethiopian, noting who initiated the encounter.*

- *What happened to Philip right after the Ethiopian's baptism (vv. 39–40)?*

- *What happened to the Ethiopian official (vv. 39–40)?*

 EXPERIENCE GOD'S HEART

Philip's extensive and productive ministry occurred because he was "full of the Holy Spirit" (6:3), wise, and obedient to the Lord Jesus Christ, his Spirit, and even angelic messengers. How about you?

- *What does it mean to be full of the Holy Spirit? Does that describe your relationship to the Spirit? If not, what do you need to ask God to do in and for you?*

- *What does it mean to be wise? Are you wise? If not, how can you move toward becoming wise?*

- *Are you obedient to God and his messengers? If so, how do you live out that obedience? If not, why?*

The Persecutor Faces the Christ

Luke now returns his account of the early church to the individual who embodied the official response of the Sanhedrin to the growing Christian movement. The man's name was Saul, and he wanted to greatly extend the persecution of Christ-followers.

Saul had agreed to the stoning of Stephen and helped launch the greatest persecution of the church in Jerusalem that believers had yet faced (8:1). This persecution that began at the center of Judaism led many Christians to flee to other places in Judea and Samaria even while the apostles chose to remain in the Jewish capital. Recognizing the flight of Christians, Saul hatched a plan to try to limit and even halt the spread of this dynamic movement. The year was likely 35.[56]

• *Read Acts 9:1–3. What was Saul's plan and motivation?*

• *When Saul was close to his destination to initiate his plan, what occurred (vv. 3–7)?*

• *When Paul finally entered Damascus, what condition was he in, and how long did he remain this way (vv. 8–9)?*

• *What happened next to fulfill what Jesus said would occur (vv. 10–19)?*

- *What indication does Luke give us to show Saul's conversion to Christ (vv. 17–18)?*

- *What did Saul do soon after his conversion and healing (vv. 20–22)?*

- *How did witnesses respond to Saul's activities (vv. 21–22)?*

- *Who plotted to kill Saul, and how did he escape them (vv. 23–25)?*

- Saul had begun his trip in Jerusalem. He had left the city a Jew committed to Judaism and extremely hostile to Christianity. When he returned to the city, he was a committed Christian who wanted his fellow Jews to know the Messiah as he now did. Read what Luke says about Saul's experience in Jerusalem and summarize your findings (vv. 26–29).

- How did Saul end up leaving Jerusalem, and where did he then go (v. 30)?

- How did the church fare after Saul became one of its most vocal and important advocates (v. 31)?

The great persecutor had become one of the persecuted. The one who had Jesus in his sights had become one of Jesus' greatest advocates. The one who had been honored and supported in Jerusalem became a target for murder while finding support among the apostles at the behest of another Christian, Barnabas. An enemy converted ended up establishing and ministering to churches all over the Mediterranean world and writing most of the books of the New Testament.

 # THE BACKSTORY

What do we know about Saul and his background? New Testament scholar Eckhard Schnabel provides a good summary:

> Saul was born in Tarsus (Acts 21:39; 22:3), the metropolis of Cilicia...The Jewish family into which he was born was devout. He was, in his own words, "circumcised on the eighth day, of the people of Israel, of the tribe of Benjamin, a Hebrew of Hebrews; in regard to the law, a Pharisee" (Phil 3:5; cf. Acts 26:5)...The description of being a "Hebrew of Hebrews" indicates that Saul was brought up speaking Hebrew and Aramaic and that the family adhered to the Jewish way of life regulated by the stipulations of the law, avoiding as much as possible assimilation to Gentile customs and maintaining contact with the Jewish community in Palestine.
>
> An expression of the family's dedication to Israel's God and his law was the fact that they belonged to the Pharisaic movement (Acts 23:6). Saul had been given the name of Israel's first king, Saul...His Roman (or Greek) name was Paul...Saul/

Paul was a Roman citizen (16:37)...Luke transitions from using the name "Saul" to "Paul" in connection with the missionary work of Saul and Barnabas on Cyprus (13:9: "Saul, also known as Paul").

Saul's native language was probably Greek, because of his early years living in Tarsus, where he and his family held citizenship (Acts 21:39). Growing up in Cilicia, he may even have understood the Cilician dialect, and he possibly spoke some Latin.

We do not know when Saul moved from Tarsus, his hometown, to Jerusalem. Paul's excellent Greek and his sovereign use of the Greek translation of the Hebrew Bible indicates that his upbringing in Tarsus must have played a major role in his education...The fact that young Saul/Paul came to Jerusalem for rabbinical studies under Rabbi Gamaliel suggests that his parents were well-to-do. This, combined with his Roman citizenship, may explain why Paul had access to the elites in the Greek and Roman cities where he preached the gospel (cf. Acts 13:4–12; 19:31).[57]

Luke will take up Saul's story again in his book of Acts, but first he will return to Peter, the leader of the apostles still residing in Jerusalem. For it will be through Peter that God will burst open the doors to the gentiles, showing that the gospel extends to all the nations and ethnic groups worldwide.

Talking It Out

1. Saul was equipped in numerous ways to become one of the church's greatest evangelists, apologists, and church planters and not only because he became filled with the Holy Spirit. What in his upbringing made him a great candidate for what God began to do through him? What in your past has also made you a good candidate for the work God has for you to do?

2. Compare Simon the sorcerer to the parable of the soils and its interpretation as told by Jesus in Luke 8:5–15. What kind of soil was Simon, and what support would you provide for your answer? How does Jesus' parable help us in our task of spreading the gospel and how we can better assess the various responses we receive to it?

3. What does this lesson help you understand about how God can use persecution and persecutors to advance his kingdom?

Part 3

Messengers to the
Rest of the World

(9:32–28:31)

LESSON 6

Peter and the Gentiles

(9:32–12:24)

Although the apostles lived in Jerusalem and ministered there, they didn't just remain there. They were active in the city and beyond it, and this included Peter, the spokesman and leader of the apostles. Moreover, other Christians were on the move, too, and wherever they went, they told others about Jesus and the good news of salvation that he brought and accomplished on the cross and through his victory over death in resurrection. So far in Luke's account, attempts to stop this movement of faith had failed. God even used the persecution of the early Christians to spread the good news farther and faster. The gospel could not be stopped!

And while the gospel was certainly good news for unbelievers, it was also good news for believers. For the one who embodied the gospel was the same one who lifted up the poor and needy, healed the ill, exorcised demons, and raised the dead. He was God in the flesh, the Son made man. And his work in human lives didn't stop with bringing people to a saving faith that delivered them just from the *penalty* of sin, which is death. He also was at work through his Spirit to deliver them from the *power* of sin and its deathly effects in their daily lives. To show this, Luke takes us back to the apostle Peter and to two incidents that occurred during his ministry near the west coast of Palestine.

Miracles for Christians

- *The first incident is recorded in Acts 9:32–35. What happened that caused the people of Lydda and Sharon to become believers?*

- *Who was Tabitha, and what was she known for among the people of Joppa (vv. 36, 39)?*

- *Describe what happened to Tabitha (v. 37). What did the believers do when they heard Peter was in Lydda? What actions did Peter take (vv. 38–41)?*

• *At the end of this episode, where did Peter stay and with whom (v. 43)?*

• *Did you notice that at the end of both accounts, each miracle resulted in many more people coming to faith in Jesus Christ? Miracles can lead to belief in the Lord. Why do you think this is so?*

• *However, for some people, even miracles are ineffective as influencers toward belief. Why do you think this also happens?*

THE BACKSTORY

So much of what happens in Acts concerns different cities, towns, and regions, not just different peoples. For example, in what we have covered so far, Aeneas, a Jewish Christian, resided in the village of Lydda, a pagan town that was "located in the midst of a rich and fertile plain."[58] This village "lay on the route from Jerusalem to the coast, about 25 miles (40 km) distant."[59] Tabitha, on the other hand, also a Christian, lived in the city of Joppa, which was "some 12 miles (19 km) from Lydda on the coast" of Palestine.[60] It served as "the port of Jerusalem."[61] Luke records such details because his account is historical. The events that occurred in and through the early church were just as real as those that occurred in, through, and around Jesus' life, death, resurrection, and ascension. We are not dealing with fiction but non-fiction, not with myth but history, not with fantasy but reality.

Cornelius—the Doorway to the Gentile World

In Acts 10:1–11:18, Luke presents a story that acts as a hinge to the rest of Acts. As New Testament scholar Darrell Bock states, "This section is one of the most important units in Acts...This scene is the book's turning point, as from here the gospel will fan out in all directions to people across a vast array of geographical regions, something Paul's three missionary journeys will underscore."[62] And it all starts with a Roman citizen and military officer—a man who symbolized the oppressive overlords of the Jewish people.

Cornelius' Vision

- *Luke introduces us to Cornelius in 10:1–2. What does he record about this man?*

Cornelius was stationed in Caesarea, a harbor city northwest of Jerusalem close to fifty miles away. The city had a temple that King Herod had built in honor of Caesar Augustus (27 BC–AD 14). Caesarea also had two aqueducts, a shrine to Mithras (the god of light), and a theater. Its population may have been as large as two hundred fifty thousand, and the city "occupied an area half the size of Manhattan Island."[63] It was also a provincial capital.

As a Roman centurion, Cornelius was "a commander of one of the six units of one hundred men within a cohort...A cohort would have had about six hundred members and would have been part of a legion of about six thousand men, which was the main division in the Roman army."[64] According to the ancient Greek historian Polybius: "Centurions are required not to be bold and adventurous so much as good leaders, of steady and prudent mind, not prone to take the offensive or start fighting wantonly, but able when overwhelmed and hard-pressed to stand fast and die at their post."[65]

- *The warrior commander Cornelius had a supernatural encounter that led him to do something he had never done before. Read verses 3–8. Describe the vision Cornelius had and how he responded to it.*

Peter's Vision and a Gospel Breakthrough

When Cornelius' men were near Joppa, the apostle Peter had a vision that perplexed him—at least for a while.

• *Just before his vision began, where was Peter, and how was he feeling (vv. 9–10)?*

• *Describe Peter's vision and how he reacted to it (vv. 10–17).*

• *Cornelius' men came into Joppa and learned where Peter was staying (v. 17). Summarize the exchange that took place between Peter and his visitors from Cornelius and what it led Peter to do (vv. 18–23). What role did the Holy Spirit play in this situation?*

- *When Peter and Cornelius' men arrived in Caesarea, who was waiting to hear Peter speak? Summarize the events, especially what Peter learned through the experience (vv. 34–48). See also study note 'k' for verse 46 and note 'a' for verse 48.*

Peter's Account Wins Support

Before Peter returned to Jerusalem from his ministry outing to the Palestinian coast, news about non-Jews "receiving God's message of new life" reached the apostles (11:1).

- *How did this news affect Peter's reception in Jerusalem (11:2)?*

- *Summarize Peter's recounting of what happened to him and Cornelius and what he concluded from it. Be sure to note new facts you learn from his recollection (vv. 4–17).*

- *How, then, did the Jewish believers in Jerusalem respond to Peter's report (v. 18)?*

As the TPT study note says: "At last the gospel broke through and penetrated into the non-Jewish cultures and people groups. The Holy Spirit was now uniting Jewish believers and non-Jewish believers into one mystical body of Christ on earth. Because of this, there would no longer be a distinction between Jew and non-Jew, but one family of believers formed by faith in Jesus Christ."[66] Or as Paul put it in Galatians: "You have all become true children of God by faith in Jesus Christ! Faith immersed you into Christ, and now you are covered and clothed with his life. And we no longer see each other in our former state—Jew or non-Jew, rich or poor, male or female—because we're all one through our union with Jesus Christ" (Galatians 3:26–28).

The Gospel and Prophecy in Antioch

With the gospel now clearly meant for gentiles, too, Luke returns to some of the consequences of the persecution that followed Stephen's execution in Jerusalem.

The Gospel Reaches to Antioch

- *Where did some believers go as the persecution grew, and what did they do as they went (Acts 11:19–21)?*

- *What was the result of the believers' ministry (v. 21–26)?*

- *Once again, Barnabas entered the picture, beginning in verse 22. What do you learn about him in this account (vv. 24–26)?*

- *What were believers in Jesus first called in Antioch (v. 26)? Also see study note 'h' for this verse.*

 THE BACKSTORY

Luke mentions three places where displaced believers traveled: Lebanon, Cyprus, and Antioch. During the first century,

Lebanon was known as Phoenicia. It was "the Mediterranean sea-coast area of Syria, with Tyre and Sidon as its main cities. It was one hundred miles long and normally fifteen miles wide."[67]

Cyprus is the third largest island in the Mediterranean Sea and lies about sixty miles west of the Syrian coastline. It was the original home of Barnabas (Acts 4:36).

Antioch, Luke's major place of focus in this part of Acts, was "the third largest city in the world at this time, coming next to Rome and Alexandria, and like them it had a large Jewish community." Antioch was known for its loose sexual morals, partially due to the ritual prostitution that took place as part of the worship of the gods Artemis and Apollo. The city was also "the seat of the provincial administration of Syria."[68]

It was in Antioch that Jesus-followers were first called Christians ("anointed ones" in TPT, 11:26). New Testament scholar and theologian Larry Hurtado explains how outsiders came to designate Jesus' followers as Christians:

> The ending of the plural form of the Greek word (*christianoi*; singular form: *christianos*) resembles the ending on the names of groups identified and aligned with this or that figure, often politically aligned groups. Note, for example, the *Herodianoi* ("Herodians") mentioned in Mark 12:13, who were likely partisans/supporters of the Herodian royal house.
>
> ...It appears that pagans who heard early believers proclaiming Jesus as *Christos* [Christ] may have taken it as some new name. Consequently, referring to believers as "Christians" may simply have designated them as people who made a figure called "Christ" such a prominent feature of their talk and their behavior. That is, it essentially designated them as partisans of this "Christ."[69]

A Prophecy of Famine

- *What also happened in Antioch about this time (Acts 11:27–30)?*

 THE BACKSTORY

The prophesied famine "was fulfilled during the reign of Claudius Caesar," writes Luke (v. 28). Claudius was the emperor of the Roman Empire from AD 41–54. According to F. F. Bruce, several historical sources report that Claudius' reign was "marked by a succession of bad harvests and serious famines in various parts of the empire." Moreover, the Jerusalem visit of "Barnabas and Saul is probably to be dated about A.D. 46,"[70] about five years into Claudius' reign. Bruce goes on to point out:

> In or about that year Judaea was hard
> hit by famine, and Josephus tells us how
> Helena, the Jewish queen-mother of
> Adiabene, east of the Tigris, bought corn in
> Egypt and figs in Cyprus at that time and
> distributed them in Jerusalem to relieve the
> hungry population.
>
> This is probably the visit to Jerusalem
> which Paul describes in Gal. 2:1 ff...If
> our identification is right, Barnabas and
> Saul took the opportunity afforded by this
> famine-relief visit to have an interview
> with the leaders of the Jerusalem church—

Peter, John, and James the Lord's brother in particular—and satisfied themselves that their status as apostles to the Gentiles was recognized by the Jerusalem apostles. Paul's statement in Gal. 2:2, that he went up to Jerusalem on that occasion "by revelation," agrees well enough with Luke's account of the prophecy of Agabus; and there is probably a direct allusion to the primary object of the visit in Gal. 2:10, which may be rendered: "Only they asked us to go on remembering their poor, and in fact I had made a special point of doing this very thing."[71]

SHARE GOD'S HEART

- *Notice that the Christians in Antioch didn't just pray for the believers in Jerusalem. Their response to the prophecy was to give what they could to provide material relief to fellow believers who would be experiencing a famine. What is your response when needs from fellow believers are shared? Is your response always to pray? Or is it to pray and then _____ (fill in the blank)? Prayer is always good, but when we can, praying plus helping to meet the need is even better. What need for another have you been praying for? What can you do to also be part of the answer to this prayer?*

Persecution, Escape, and Judgment

Moving back to Jerusalem and Judea, Luke returns to another persecution of the church, this time led by Herod Agrippa I, the "King Herod" whom Luke mentions (Acts 12:1). Agrippa was born in 10 BC, the grandson of Herod the Great, who died in 4 BC. Agrippa's father was executed in 7 BC, after which he was raised by his mother in Rome where he got to know the imperial family.

> In his youth he was something of a playboy, and in A.D. 23 he went so heavily into debt that he had to flee to Idumea to escape his creditors. Later he received asylum at Tiberius and a pension from his uncle Herod Antipas, with whom, however, he eventually quarreled. In 36 he returned to Rome but offended the emperor Tiberius and was imprisoned. At the death of Tiberius in 37, he was released by the new emperor Caligula and received from him the northernmost Palestinian tetrarchies of Philip and Lysanias (cf. Luke 3:1) and the title of king. When Herod Antipas was banished in 39, Agrippa received his tetrarchy as well. At the death of Caligula in 41, Claudius, who succeeded Caligula and was Agrippa's friend from youth, added Judea and Samaria to his territory, thus reconstituting for him the entire kingdom of his grandfather Herod the Great, over which he ruled till his death in 44.[72]

King Agrippa worked hard to win the affection of the Jews he ruled. Not a Jew himself, "when in Jerusalem, he acted the part of an observant Jew," careful to follow the Jewish rituals and other traditions. "When Judea came under his jurisdiction, he moved the seat of government from Caesarea to Jerusalem. This established the holy city in Jewish eyes as the political capital of the country. He also began to rebuild the city's northern wall and fortifications, thus enhancing both its security and its prestige." He was effective at supporting the Jewish majority in the lands under his control, and he "ruthlessly suppressed minorities when they became disruptive."[73] One of these minority groups was the Christians, and it was the Jewish authorities in Jerusalem who particularly found them offensive.

- *What did King Herod Agrippa I do against the Christians in Jerusalem, and how did the church there respond (Acts 12:1–5; see also study note 'd')?*

- *The apostle Jacob, also known as James, was the first martyr among the apostles, executed in AD 44.[74] Turn to Mark 10:35–39 and read what Jesus told him and his brother. Did Jesus' prophetic word come true?[75]*

- *How did Agrippa attempt to ensure that Peter would remain in his custody (v. 6)?*

- *Describe how this attempt failed (vv. 7–11).*

- *Where did Peter go, what did he do, and how was he received (vv. 12–17)?*

- *What did King Agrippa do after he learned that Peter was no longer in prison (vv. 18–19)?*

- *Luke tells us about King Agrippa's last days (vv. 20–23). Summarize what Luke says about the king and why this ruler met such a hideous end.*

- *After Agrippa's death, how did the church fare (v. 24)?*

EXPERIENCE GOD'S HEART

Peter and the believers praying for him were all stunned that the apostle had been freed from his imprisonment. Had they prayed? Yes. Did they believe that God could free their beloved leader? Yes. Did they believe that God would deliver him? Ahh. There's no indication in the text that any of them presumed upon the will of God. God can do anything, including the humanly impossible. But will he perform a specific action in a certain situation when his people pray? Is God like a vending machine, such that we can pop in a prayer, push our selection, and always receive our choice when we want it? No, he's nothing like that. Even the early believers of the church knew this, which is why they were all surprised when God freed Peter in response to their prayers. Even Peter was taken aback by what God did for him.

We can count on God always being for us and with us. But how God will specifically respond in any given situation? That is beyond our pay grade. God sees the whole picture of our lives. We see but part, and we often don't see that clearly. We must trust that God knows what is best, not just for the short-term but for the long-term as well, and not just for us but also for everyone whose lives will be touched by ours, perhaps even well after we have joined Jesus in heaven.

So being surprised by what God does in response to our prayers is one of many proper responses. What we must never do is assume that God must act in a specific way in any given situation. That's the sin of presumption. God is much wiser and smarter than we are. We should never forget that.

- *Have you ever been surprised, even stunned, by how God answered one of your prayers or the prayer of someone you know? If so, describe what happened.*

- *Is there something you need and are looking to God to supply? Are you willing to trust him to decide what to do for you in this situation? If not, why?*

- *Have you ever prayed for something you did not then receive? If so, what, if anything, did you receive instead? Did God's response turn out to be better for you or perhaps for someone else? Explain what happened and what you learned from it.*

Talking It Out

1. Today we take it for granted that the gospel is for all peoples, but Christians have not always understood or even applied this truth. Discuss what might hinder presenting the gospel to individuals of different nationalities, ethnicities, cultures, and religions. How can we overcome these hindrances?

2. Luke makes it clear that the advancement of the gospel occurred under the guidance and power of the Holy Spirit. Is that still true today? If so, in what ways have you or others you know perceived this?

3. God's enemies face his judgment, not always immediately but always sometime. Scripture repeatedly testifies to this fact, as does church history. Bible scholar John Stott rightly says: "Tyrants may be permitted for a time to boast and bluster, oppressing the church and hindering the spread of the gospel, but they will not last. In the end, their empire will be broken and their pride abased."[76] What wicked rulers from biblical history or beyond can you name who illustrate this point? How has this truth helped believers when they have faced tyranny in their lives? How do you think it would help you?

LESSON 7

Paul's First Missionary Journey

(12:25–15:35)

After King Herod Agrippa's death, the Christian movement continued to grow. And its most fruitful missionary was Saul, the former persecutor whom Christians had feared so much. The rest of the book of Acts centers primarily on Saul's activities on behalf of his Savior and Lord, Jesus the Christ. Soon the church came to know Saul as Paul as he traveled throughout the Roman Empire from Jerusalem in the east to Rome in the west and many places in between. He may have even made it as far west as Spain (but Acts doesn't cover his travels that far; more about that in the last lesson).

Saul the persecutor became Paul the preacher.

Saul the Pharisee became Paul the Christian.

Saul the defender of Judaism became Paul the advocate for Christ.

Paul's missionary travels helped fulfill Jesus' directive to his apostles to be his messengers of the gospel to "the distant provinces—even to the remotest places on earth!" (Acts 1:8).

The Devil in Cyprus

Barnabas had been Saul's advocate soon after the Pharisee's conversion, supporting Saul before the apostles in Jerusalem (9:26–27). Now Luke reports that Barnabas accompanied Saul to Jerusalem, taking the money fellow believers had raised for those

Christians who needed relief from the famines hitting the area (12:25). "Whereas Agrippa died in A.D. 44, a probable date for the famine-relief visit of Barnabas and Paul is A.D. 46."[77] A disciple named Mark (also known as John) traveled with Saul and Barnabas from Jerusalem back to Antioch, the capital of Syria. Mark was a cousin of Barnabas (Colossians 4:10) who lived in Jerusalem with his mother (Acts 12:12).

- *While the three missionaries were in Antioch, what happened (Acts 13:1–3)?*

 THE BACKSTORY

Luke mentions several prophets and teachers who were part of the church in Antioch (13:1). Barnabas, of course, is someone we've encountered before in Luke's history of the early church. Barnabas was "a Greek-speaking Jew from Cyprus who had lived in Jerusalem" (Acts 4:36–37).[78] He became a respected leader of the church in Antioch, Syria (11:22–26).

Simeon "may have been a black man of African origin as his grecized Latin name 'Niger'...suggests, a term that means 'dark-complexioned' or 'black.'"[79]

"Lucius the Libyan" was also from Africa. Before he became a believer in Jesus, he may have been a member of the synagogue in Jerusalem that initially opposed Stephen (6:9).

Manean, who is identified as a "childhood companion of King Herod Antipas" (13:1), was likely from a "noble Jewish family with connections to Herod's court." One scholar suggests that Manean, "before his conversion, may have held an influential position at the court of Herod Antipas."[80]

Saul, of course, was a converted Jew from Tarsus who had studied under rabbi Gamaliel in Jerusalem, had supported Stephen's stoning, had persecuted believers in Judea, and then, after his conversion to Christ, became a missionary active in Damascus, Nabatea, and Cilicia before working with fellow Christians in Antioch (7:58; 9:20–22, 30; 11:25–26).

- *At the direction of the Holy Spirit, the Antiochene leaders sent Saul, Barnabas, and John Mark off to fulfill what God wanted them to do. Where did these three men go first, and what did they do (13:4–5)? (Follow Paul's first missionary journey using the map in TPT titled "The Mission of Paul and Barnabas.")*

Their first stop on the island of Cyprus was Salamis. Before an earthquake devastated the city in 15 BC, it had been the island's seat of government. Although Caesar Augustus rebuilt the city, the government offices moved to Paphos, which was on the western side of the island. The three missionaries traveled from Salamis to Paphos, stopping along the way to engage in Christian ministry in the synagogues. Paphos, as the capital of the province, was a "typical Greco-Roman city with the usual infrastructure that included numerous temples, a theater, an amphitheater, a *gymnasion*, baths, and also a mint."[81]

- *Whom did Saul, Barnabas, and John Mark encounter in Paphos? What was this man's reputation? What happened when he tried to prevent the governor of Paphos from hearing the gospel (13:6–12)?*

- *What in the text indicates that this encounter involved spiritual warfare? In the battle, which side won?*

- *Review what Paul says about the armor God provides us for engaging in spiritual conflict (Ephesians 6:11–18). Which aspects of this armor are evident in what occurred in Paphos?*

The Case for Jesus as Messiah

- *After their time in Paphos, Cyprus, where did Paul, Barnabas, and John Mark go? Where did John Mark then travel to (vv. 13–14)?*

The Antioch here is not the same city as the Antioch in Syria. This Antioch was in the region of Pisidia in what we know today as Turkey but what was then called Asia. Pisidian Antioch was "a civil and military center...the leading city of the region."[82] It had a large Jewish population. According to Josephus, two thousand Jewish families resided in the region.[83] While in this city, Paul and Barnabas engaged with "seven different social levels of people: synagogue officials, Jews, proselytes, God-fearers, devout women of high standing, Gentiles, and leading men of the city. Their message penetrates all levels of society."[84]

- *On a Sabbath day, Paul and Barnabas entered a synagogue in Pisidian Antioch. Who invited them to speak? Which of the men stood and addressed those in attendance? Summarize what prologue he gave to speaking about Jesus (vv. 14–22).*

- *What did Paul then say about Jesus (vv. 23–25)?*

- *Whom did he say condemned Jesus to death and why? Did these people still, even through this injustice, fulfill God's Word (vv. 26–29)?*

- *Through what event did God vindicate Jesus, and what prophecy did that fulfill (vv. 30–37)?*

- *What is now available through Jesus (vv. 38–39)?*

- *What warning did Paul leave with his audience (vv. 40–41)?*

- *What happened as Paul and Barnabas began leaving the synagogue (vv. 42–43)?*

- *On the following Sabbath, how did the Jewish leaders react when Paul and Barnabas returned to the synagogue? After the Jews rejected the gospel, who joyfully received the message Paul and Barnabas presented (vv. 44–49)?*

- *Under what circumstances did Paul and Barnabas leave Pisidian Antioch (vv. 50–51)?*

- *Even as they traveled to Iconium, what were the new Christian converts doing in Pisidian Antioch (v. 52)?*

- *Why do you think Paul and Barnabas were driven out of the city by some of the Jewish religious leaders and upper-class citizens?*

Confrontation in Iconium

Iconium was ninety miles southeast of Pisidian Antioch. The city was "located at the juncture of several important roads," and it was the most important judicial center "where the governors regularly heard legal cases."[85]

- *What did Paul and Barnabas do in Iconium that they regularly did elsewhere, and what kind of crowd did they draw (14:1)?*

- *What opposition did these missionaries face? What successes did they achieve and why (vv. 2–3)?*

- *What led to these Christian leaders eventually leaving Iconium (vv. 4–6)?*

Worldview Clash in Lystra

After Paul and Barnabas left Iconium, they traveled to the "region of Lyconia, to the cities of Lystra and Derbe" (v. 6). These two cities, while not the only ones in the region, virtually controlled the territory of Lyconia. "Lystra was about 20 miles (34 km.) southwest of Iconium, and Derbe was 93 miles (150 km.) east of Lystra."[86]

- *What did Paul and Barnabas do in Lyconia (v. 7)?*

- *While ministering in the city of Lystra, what miracle did Paul perform (vv. 8–10)?*

- *Read verses 11–18 and summarize the response this miracle provoked in the crowd that witnessed it.*

- *How did Paul and Barnabas attempt to change the crowd's perception of what had happened (vv. 14–17)?*

- *Despite Paul's pleas, the people continued to wrongly interpret the miracle they had seen. How did the Jewish leaders from Antioch and Iconium take advantage of this situation (vv. 18–21)?*

⚡ DIGGING DEEPER

What happened in Lystra was a clash of worldviews. A worldview is the lens through which we interpret our world. Like a pair of colored glasses, our worldview colors how we see and experience what we encounter. Paul and Barnabas were Christian theists. They saw the healing miracle as a work of the living God who created all things, who has provided ample evidence of his existence and goodness, and who is for human flourishing. Only he is God; there is no other. However, the crowd who witnessed this miracle was filled with pagan polytheists. Polytheists believe in many gods, not just one, and they mistook Barnabas to be the god Zeus and Paul to be the god Hermes—ancient Greek gods who had limited spheres of authority and existed with many other gods. Zeus was regarded as the chief god among the other gods, and Hermes, a son of Zeus, was the messenger of his fellow gods.

The audience of the miracle saw Paul and Barnabas through the polytheistic lens of their worldview and thereby determined that these individuals must be gods appearing in human form. Paul and Barnabas rightly saw the worldview clash and attempted to counter it with the truth of Christian theism, but worldviews are usually deeply rooted and are not easily put aside—a fact Paul and Barnabas experienced through the crowd's frenetic response to what the one real God had done to confirm the gospel message.

Nevertheless, as hard as it is to overcome false worldviews, Paul and Barnabas did, "winning a large number of followers to Jesus" (v. 21). Of course, their ministry was supernaturally empowered, and the conversions to Jesus were also the fruit of God's work in the lives of the unconverted. The one true God had overcome the false gods of polytheism. Theism triumphed over "worthless myths" (v. 15).[87]

⚘ EXPERIENCE GOD'S HEART

So far in Acts, we have seen the apostles arrested, imprisoned, beaten, lied about, misidentified, left for dead, run out of town...and the list goes on. They paid a high price for following Jesus and obeying him. And what did they receive in return? They witnessed miraculous healings, conversions to Jesus and everlasting life, supernatural liberation from prison, exceeding joy in the Lord, wonderful acts of sacrifice and charity, various ethnicities coming together in unity in Christ, many of their fellow Jews embracing the Messiah...and on that list goes. While the cost of following Christ can be high, the rewards are greater still.

- *What have you sacrificed and endured for the sake of your identity with and obedience to Jesus Christ?*

- *What have you received in return?*

- *Given the cost of being a Christian, would you still encourage others to come to know Jesus personally and to accept him by faith? Why?*

♥ SHARE GOD'S HEART

Worldviews are shaped and informed by one's answers to life's big questions, such as: Does a God exist? If so, what is the divine reality like? Did the universe come to be? If so, how? What is truth, and how can we know it? Can we know what is right and wrong? If so, how? What is a human being? How did we originate? Do we have a purpose, and if so, what is it? And where are we and history headed? These are heady questions, and answering them is not easy.

For example, answers to the first two questions lead to at least seven different conceptions of God, with one worldview—*atheism*—denying that any God exists. *Polytheism* says that many gods exist, perhaps even an infinite number of deities, and all of them are finite (limited in some way). *Pantheism* says that God is the world and the world is God. God is all there is; everything else is mere shadow, maybe even illusory. *Panentheism* claims that God is greater than the world and that the world is God's body. God can become more than he is right now, and as he develops, he persuades the world to grow with him. Another worldview, *deism*, argues that God is distinct from the world. He created the world and may even sustain it in existence, but he does not involve himself in history or in human affairs. From this view, there are no miracles. There are still other worldviews, but these are enough to show how many different ways humans can and have conceived the divine.

• *Do you know someone who holds a different worldview than you do? If so, what is it, and how would that person answer some or all the big questions previously mentioned?*

• *Do you know the Christian worldview well enough that you could answer some or all those big questions listed earlier? If so, take at least two of those questions and sketch out your answers to them.*

• *Now consider how you would share your worldview with someone who doesn't accept it. Recall how hard it can be to hear about a worldview that's foreign to the listener and the possible misunderstandings that can arise. How can you clear up misunderstandings in a respectful yet honest way?*

Equipping Believers

Paul and Barnabas "retraced their steps and revisited Lystra, Iconium, and [Pisidian] Antioch" (Acts 14:21).

- *What did these Christian leaders do during this part of the travels (vv. 22–23)?*

- *What was the very last leg of their journey? Where did they go, and what did they do before returning to Syrian Antioch (vv. 24–26)?*

- *Once they were back to their home base of Syrian Antioch, what did these leaders do (vv. 26–28)?*

Finding refreshment with fellow believers after a demanding missionary journey (likely from AD 48 to 49[88]) must have renewed the hearts and minds of Paul and Barnabas. We can imagine how their report of all that happened on their journey must have encouraged and inspired the Christians in Antioch. Rest is good for the soul.

- *Do you find times of rest and refreshment after working hard, especially if the project lasted many weeks, not just several days? Rest is something God wants us to do. None of us has inexhaustible energy or drive. We all need renewal. This is why Jesus noted that God's Sabbath rest was designed for us, not us for the Sabbath (Mark 2:27; cf. Exodus 20:8–11). That is, God knows we need rest. He didn't command the Sabbath simply for us to have something to obey. He commanded it for our benefit. How do you take time to rest and relax, to renew your depleted energy? If rest is not part of your routine, why not?*

The First Church Council

Throughout church history, Christian leaders have gathered at councils to hash through issues and make decisions intended to maintain church unity on doctrine and practice and to clearly lay out what the Christian faith teaches on key matters, especially in response to serious doctrinal errors (heresies) that divide Christians and undermine basic truths. Some of these councils have clarified key doctrines, such as the Trinity and the incarnation. Those councils have benefited the church for centuries. Other councils, however, failed to achieve their stated goals, and some of them made decisions that went far beyond and even counter to what Scripture teaches. So the history of councils in the church has been a mixed bag of help and hurt.[89] But the idea of leaders gathering in a council to hash out divisive controversies is rooted in the very first church council, which took place in Jerusalem in the year 49 under the supervision of the apostles. And this council's decision has been definitive for the church worldwide for two thousand years now. Luke tells us about it in Acts 15.

- *While Paul and Barnabas were still in Antioch, Syria, who came to town, and what was their purpose (Acts 15:1–2)?*

- *What did the church leaders in Antioch do to resolve the issue (vv. 2–3)?*

- *Whom did Paul and Barnabas meet with in Jerusalem, and what was the issue raised (vv. 4–5)?*

- *After some lengthy discussion, who stood up to speak to the other assembled church leaders, and what was his response to the issue at hand (vv. 6–10)?*

- *Paul and Barnabas then spoke up. What did they share with the group (v. 12)? How did that bear on the issue under discussion?*

- *The last speaker was Jacob, the brother of Jesus (see 1 Corinthians 15:7 and the study note on that verse). He had become the chief leader of the Jerusalem church. What did he say about the issue under discussion, and what decision did he think the apostles and elders should make on it (Acts 15:13–21)?*

- Who chose delegates to take the Jerusalem council's decision back to the church in Antioch? Who were the chosen delegates? And what did they take with them (vv. 22–23)?

- Read verses 23–29. What was the council's decision as expressed in the letter, and how does it compare to what Jacob recommended the council do?

- In Syrian Antioch, how did the church receive the council's written decision, and how did they treat the delegates? Who stayed in Antioch, and what did they do there (vv. 30–35)?

- *All in all, how would you assess the effectiveness of the first church council? Did it accomplish what it had intended?*

- *Have you been in a situation that raised controversy over Christian belief or practice? If so, what was the issue at stake? Was it ever resolved? If so, how? What did you learn through the experience?*

During Paul's first missionary journey, his continual companion was Barnabas, and their practice was to go to the synagogues in the towns and cities they visited, giving Jews the gospel message first. But they did not neglect reaching out to non-Jews (gentiles). And whether they presented the gospel to Jews or gentiles, the response was always mixed: some people believed, and others did not. And among those who didn't accept Jesus as Savior and Lord, some became downright hostile and even tried to kill the missionary pair. But God kept working through these two men and the many other Christians who shared their faith wherever they went. The church kept growing in number, sins were forgiven, bodies were healed, relationships were reconciled, and hope and joy increased. Trouble was still never far away, but God and his Word were greater still.

Talking It Out

1. The fact that a church council met to settle an issue indicates that truth was at stake and that it mattered. Discuss why it's essential to live according to what is true rather than what is false, including and especially the truths of the Christian faith.

2. Luke tells us about the courage and boldness of Paul and Barnabas, especially in the face of opposition (Acts 13:45–46; 14:3, 19–20; 15:2). What is your posture when your Christian faith is challenged? Do you engage critics? Do you stand up for Jesus? Why or why not?

3. No missionary effort is 100 percent effective. Not everyone who hears the gospel responds to it by faith. Even the apostles could not win universal acceptance of it. Talk about why this is so and what it tells us about human nature and what our evangelistic expectations should be.

LESSON 8

Paul's Second Missionary Journey

(15:36–18:22)

Obedient to the Lord, Paul continued to take the good news of salvation in Christ to those who had not yet heard the message. He also returned to places he had already been so he could build up believers in the faith, deepening their roots in the rich soil of Christian belief and practice. Along the way, he encountered what he had on his first missionary journey: conversions to Christ, disbelief and criticism, and outright antagonism. Even before the second journey began, a disagreement broke up a successful team while leading to a new arrangement that saw successes too.

A Falling Out

- *Before the second missionary journey began, what did Paul and Barnabas disagree about, and how did they resolve the matter (Acts 15:36–40)?*

• *Have you ever been the subject of contention between two parties, or do you know someone who has? Why did the issue come up, and how was it resolved? Were there any lingering consequences? If so, what were the consequences, and did the parties ever address them?*

Conflict is a matter of life, and it can occur regardless of one's position of authority, leadership, influence, or experience. Two men who had worked together, evangelized and defended the faith together, and suffered together had a falling out over a fellow believer, John Mark, a cousin of Barnabas (Colossians 4:10). Barnabas wanted John Mark to travel with them; Paul did not. The disagreement was so intense that the two leaders decided to keep serving but separately. Barnabas traveled west to Cyprus with John Mark, the island on which Barnabas lived (Acts 4:36–37). Paul chose Silas as his new companion. Silas was a prophet and part of the delegation that had taken the Jerusalem council's written decision to Antioch (15:25–27, 30–32). He was also a Roman citizen (16:37–38), as Paul was. He had stayed in Antioch with Paul and Barnabas and ministered to the church with them. He was a known and proven asset.[90]

All that we know about the problem involving John Mark was that he had "deserted" Paul and Barnabas during their first missionary journey, "leaving them to do their missionary work without him" (15:38). Why John Mark left the team, we're not told. Apparently, however, Paul wasn't convinced of John Mark's staying power in missionary work, so he refused to have him join the team again. What we do know, however, is that Paul and John Mark later reconciled, and Paul even came to regard him as "a tremendous help" in his ministry (2 Timothy 4:11).

- *Have you ever had a strained relationship with someone you worked or performed ministry with? How did that come about? How did that disagreement affect your ability to do your job? Did any reconciliation ever take place?*

- *Is there anything you would do differently if such a conflict ever occurred again? What might that be?*

- *The believers in Syrian Antioch showed their support for the new Paul-Silas team. How did they do this (Acts 15:40)?*

- *What was the initial success of this team (v. 41)? (You can follow this entire missionary journey by using the map titled "Paul's Second Missionary Journey" in TPT.)*

DIGGING DEEPER

Silas was Paul's replacement for Barnabas, and the church at Syrian Antioch approved of his choice (Acts 15:40). Silas proved to be a good traveling and ministry companion for Paul. Silas and Paul brought the gospel to Syria and Turkey, including the cities of Derbe and Lystra (16:1). In Macedonia and after they picked up Timothy for their team, they ministered in Philippi (v. 12), Thessalonica (17:1, 4), Berea (v. 10), and Corinth (18:1, 5; 2 Corinthians 1:19). And Silas suffered with Paul at least in Philippi (Acts 16:19–24).

In the New Testament, Silas is also referred to as Silvanus. "Silvanus is a Latin name; Silas may have been a friendly abbreviation of it."[91] It's also possible that, like Paul, Silas went by two names for another reason: Silvanus was his Latin and formal name, and Silas was his Jewish name.

Silas is also mentioned in 1 Peter 5:12 as assisting Peter in writing that letter. F. F. Bruce suggests that Silas "was probably the amanuensis employed in the writing down of 1 Peter, and responsible for its rather elegant Greek style; it may also have been he who carried the letter to the various provinces in Asia Minor where the addressees lived (1 Pet. 1:1)."[92]

Another New Partner

- *After Paul and Silas arrived in Lystra, they added another member to their team. Who was it, and what does Luke tell us about him, including what Paul required of him (16:1–3)?*

- *Why do you think it was so important to Paul that Timothy be circumcised?*

- *How effective was this ministry team of three (vv. 4–5)?*

 DIGGING DEEPER

Paul's new partner Timothy proved to be a great ministry partner. For example, Paul mentioned him at the start of several of his letters (2 Corinthians 1:1; Colossians 1:1; 1 Thessalonians 1:1; 2 Thessalonians 1:1; Philemon 1). "This does not mean," writes Bruce, "that Timothy had any responsible share in the composition of the letter. He may have taken down the letter at Paul's dictation, but Paul does not give a man a place alongside himself in the superscription just because he was his amanuensis...Timothy's name is associated with his own because Timothy shared his ministry on a permanent footing." Bruce adds, "Of all members of Paul's circle, there was none with whom he formed a closer mutual attachment than Timothy."[93]

- *So what did Paul see in Timothy that led him to choose him and continue to work with him for years to come? To answer this, look up the Scripture passages in the left-hand column in the following chart, and then to the right of each passage, jot down what Paul says about Timothy. Then reflect on Timothy's character and utility and ask yourself if he had any traits that you have or would like to have in your life. Take your reflections to God in prayer.*

Paul's View of Timothy

Scripture	Timothy's Traits
Romans 16:21	
1 Corinthians 4:17	
1 Corinthians 16:10	
Philippians 2:19	
1 Thessalonians 3:2	
1 Thessalonians 3:6	
1 Timothy 1:2	
1 Timothy 1:18	

Course Changes

• *Read Acts 16:6–10, and then answer the following questions:*

Who blocked the Pauline team's way to certain places of possible ministry?

For what possible reasons do you think God would close doors to the gospel, at least temporarily?

Did Paul and his team obey the divine directives? What led them to believe that Macedonia had been opened for them to engage in ministry?

Have you ever had a divine vision? Whether you have or not, what ways has God used to guide your steps? How did you know that it was God who was directing you?

In verse 10, the personal pronoun shifts from third-person plural to first-person plural, from "they" to "we." This indicates that Luke had joined Paul's team, traveling with them to Macedonia. So now the team consisted of Paul, Silas, Timothy, and Luke.

Philippi

According to Bible scholar Daryl Bock:

> Macedonia, located in northern Greece, was bordered by the Illyria and Nestos rivers. Macedonia had been a world power under Philip of Macedonia and Alexander the Great four centuries earlier. Since 168 BC it had been a Roman province. The Greeks regarded the Macedonians as barbarians, except for the royal family, but they shared the same gods as the Greeks. Philippi became its principal city during the Roman period.[94]

Once in Macedonia, Paul's team traveled to Philippi. It was a wealthy city, "rich with copper, silver, and gold deposits." It was also a "Roman colony, which made it legally like a Roman city. It had an autonomous government, freedom from tribute and taxation, and legal-ownership rights."[95] Archaeological work there has found that 80 percent of the inscriptions on statues, buildings, and so on are in Latin, which indicates the primary Roman and gentile character of the city. The Jewish presence there must have been small.

- *"When the Sabbath day came" (Acts 16:13), what did Paul's team do? Whom did they meet? What was she like? How did she respond to the gospel (vv. 13–15)?*

- *Still in Philippi, Paul and his companions picked up an unwelcome follower. Who was this person, and how did she bother them (vv. 16–18; also see study note 'a' on verse 16)?*

- *How did Paul finally deal with the irritant, and what trouble did it bring him and Silas (vv. 18–22)?*

- *Profit loss from the formerly demon-possessed girl began the outrage against Paul and Silas, but what accusations did the slave girl's owners level against them when they forced Paul and Silas to appear before the city's magistrates (vv. 20–21)? Why do you think the complaint shifted from money to religion? How were the two matters closely related in a city full of idolatry and its practices?*

•

- *Where did the two missionaries end up, and how did they respond to their situation (vv. 23–25)?*

- *What happened during the middle of the night that led to the proliferation of the gospel (vv. 26–34)?*

- *Summarize how the entire ordeal came to an end (vv. 35–40).*

- *Why do you think Paul pushed the matter of the violation of his and Silas' rights as Roman citizens? Why didn't he just let the matter go?*

Thessalonica

Apparently, Timothy and Luke stayed behind in Philippi. Luke tells us that it was only Paul and Silas who left the city and traveled on to the city of Thessalonica.

Thessalonica "was the capital of the province of Macedonia, which [the Roman emperor] Claudius had reorganized in AD 44." The city's population was "between 40,000 and 65,000," and it was governed by "a group of five or six magistrate officials called politarchs."[96] Traveling from Philippi, it would have taken Paul and Silas about three days to make the seventy-mile journey if they rode on horses; otherwise, foot travel would have added another few days. This was due to the ruggedness of the route along the coast, "which went from shore to hills almost immediately." Thessalonica served as a "vital link to the Balkans with routes by land and sea." The city also had a "major harbor and was a key link to the Bosporus and the Black Sea."[97] It was ideally situated for the flow of commerce and people.

- *While in this metropolis, what did Paul and Silas do, and was it something that was normal or abnormal for them (17:1–3)?*

- *What was the people's response to the missionaries' message, both positive and negative (vv. 4–9)? What charges did the mob bring to the magistrates (city council)?*

- *Why do you think the gospel message and the claim that Jesus was the Messiah sparked so much controversy and hostility?*

WORD WEALTH

The word translated "bail" (v. 9) "refers to the taking of 'legal security' or bail, something to guarantee that this missionary group will not break the Roman law."[98] In this case, bail apparently required that, in return for the release of Jason and the believers with him, they had to send Paul and Silas out of the city to ensure no more trouble would erupt. This fits with Paul's remarks in 1 Thessalonians 2:14–18.[99]

Berea

From Thessalonica, Paul and Silas traveled to Berea (v. 10). It was an out-of-the-way town that the ancient Roman historian Livy called "noble." Berea was forty-five miles southwest of Thessalonica, and it sat on a slope overlooking the Haliacmon River.[100] Luke indicates that Timothy joined the two men in Berea (v. 14). Apparently, Luke was still not with the team, for the third-person plural pronouns are still in use at this point in Acts.

- *Paul and Silas had a very different experience in Berea than they had in Thessalonica, at least initially. What was different in Berea, and what is Luke's explanation for it (vv. 10–12)?*

- *Who brought this great response to an end, and how did they do it (v. 13)?*

- *What did this opposition lead Paul, Silas, and Timothy to do (vv. 14–15)?*

 EXPERIENCE GOD'S HEART

The Jews' reception of Paul in Berea is a model of how to be responsive to God's Word. They were "open minded," "hungry to learn," and "eagerly received the word." When they opened the Scriptures, which they did daily, they searched and examined them "to verify that what Paul taught them was true" (17:11). Why were they this way? It began with their character, of which Luke says that they were "noble" (v. 11). Their character led them to remain open to what God's Word taught, to examine it so as to test Paul's interpretation of Scripture. As a result, a considerable number of Jews, as well as some "influential Greek women and men," came to Christ (v. 12).

The Bible can withstand human scrutiny. After all, it is God's Word, infallible in all it teaches. It is true because its ultimate

Author is the source of truth (John 14:6; 15:26; 1 John 4:6), and he cannot lie (Titus 1:2; Hebrews 6:18). We can barrage Scripture with our questions, approach it with our doubts, and search its pages for the truth we seek. As long as we approach his Word as the Bereans did, with the character and intellectual openness that they exhibited, we will find answers—answers that will feed us, sustain us, empower us, and equip us until we finally come fully into the presence of he who is the Truth.

- *What questions and doubts do you have about what Scripture teaches?*

- *What is your posture to God's Word? Are you open to what it teaches, or are you predisposed to reject it? Are you willing to dig for answers, or do you tend to give up when the answers don't come quickly and easily? Search your heart and mind and ask the God of truth to create in you the character and mindset that will persistently seek answers and remain open to receive and embrace whatever those answers are.*

Athens

Athens was a famous city in the Mediterranean world. It was the center of philosophy, boasting the likes of Socrates, Plato, Aristotle, Epicurus, and Zeno. While part of the Roman Empire, it was a decidedly Greek city with a learned and democratic past. Some of the most beautiful buildings in the empire could be found there, among them the Parthenon, which was the temple of Athena, the city's patron goddess. The Parthenon housed a magnificent statue of the goddess. One could also find the Theater of Dionysus, a god of fertility, wine, and ecstasy. Throughout the city were statues of men and women as well as gods and goddesses, such as Zeus, Hermes, and Apollo. While Rome "left the city free politically to carry on her own institutions as a free city within the empire," the population of Athens had considerably dwindled by Paul's day, perhaps as low as ten thousand.[101]

- *What was Paul's assessment of Athens, and where did he go to present and defend the gospel (vv. 16–17)?*

- *Who were the two groups of philosophers Paul especially engaged? What did they believe, and how did they respond to Paul's message (vv. 18–21; see also notes 'g' and 'h' for verse 18)?*

Paul was brought before "the leadership council of Athens" (vv. 19, 22). This was "the senate or city council" of Athens. It was a council of city administrators, "the chief judicial body of the city" that "exercised jurisdiction in such matters as religion and education."[102] This council was tasked to hear what Paul had to say so they could continue to give him the freedom to speak in the city, censor him, or silence him.

- *When Paul arose to speak to this council, what did he say to establish some common ground and create some curiosity in the case he was about to bring (vv. 22–23)?*

- *Recall that Athens was full of idols to false deities. Given that, to what subject did Paul go to begin the substance of his presentation? What did he say about this "true God" (vv. 24–28)?*

- *How else did he distance the true God from the false gods represented all over Athens (v. 29)? On what basis did he make this claim—that is, what facts had Paul already presented that logically led away from accepting idols as gods?*

- *Read verses 30–31. What did Paul say God now commanded of them? Why was now the time?*

When Paul mentioned the Savior's resurrection from the dead, his presentation came to an abrupt end. Some people mocked him and left, others thought he might be worth hearing some more, and some became believers (v. 32). Many Greeks believed in the immortality of the soul, while other Greeks thought that death was the end of the line, that there was no life after death. No one thought the body worthy of resurrection. They considered that notion to be absurd.

Still, Luke mentions that among those who believed Paul's message was one of the judges on the leadership council, a man named Dionysius, and a woman named Damaris (v. 34). The conversion number may not have been large enough to mention, but some individuals did accept Christ.

Nevertheless, Paul did not stay in Athens, and, except for

Luke's account, there's no sign that a church of any significance took root there during Paul's lifetime. However, F. F. Bruce states:

> Athens was in due course to embrace wholeheartedly the message which he [Paul] brought. The text of his address to the Areopagus is engraved on a bronze tablet at the foot of the ascent to the hill. A thoroughfare west of the hill is called 'Street of the Apostle Paul,' and running off it towards the east, on the south side of the Acropolis, is the 'Street of Dionysius the Areopagite' (Paul's principal Athenian convert). Paul would be surprised, but no doubt gratified, could he know that his visit and preaching have been so well remembered.[103]

♥ SHARE GOD'S HEART

When you are dealing with individuals who know little about Christianity, Paul's presentation in Athens can serve as a working model for how to proceed.

First, Paul began by expressing respect for his audience (17:22). People are much more inclined to listen when they are treated respectfully.

Second, Paul found something in their belief and practice that he could speak about positively. He acknowledged their religious devotion as a good thing. While it was certainly misdirected to false gods, they at least had an altar to "The Unknown God"—a point of reverence that Paul could then take to direct his audience to the one true God (v. 23). We can always find something in what someone else believes or does that we can affirm and even build upon. This allows us to first affirm whom we are speaking to rather than starting with criticism, which hardly anyone finds easy to take.

Third, Paul began and developed the substance of his talk with the most important doctrine of all—the reality, nature, and activity of the one true God (vv. 24–31). Through that doctrine, he also affirmed a number of facts about human beings:

- *Our life comes from God; we are completely dependent on him (v. 25).*

- *We were created by God, beginning with one man, Adam (v. 26).*

- *Since we have a common origin, we are related by creation (v. 26).*

- *God sets our distribution and times in history (v. 26).*

- *God has designed us to seek him and find him (v. 27).*

- *Our very human nature comes from God (v. 28).*

- *God has been gracious and merciful to us (v. 30).*

- *The human race should repent of its unworthy notions of God and turn to him (v. 30).*

- *All of us are accountable to God and will be judged by him (v. 30).*

- *God has chosen a man and raised him from the dead as verification of these facts about God and us (v. 31).*

In Paul's presentation, he began with God, moved to humankind, and emphasized God's relationship to us from creation to redemption before he even mentioned bodily resurrection—the critical sticking point for his largely Greek audience. Paul laid out the foundational beliefs of the Christian faith before he began to present the historical facts about Jesus and what he accomplished for all human beings. While Paul's speech was cut short, imagine how little he would have been able to present if he had started with Jesus' crucifixion and resurrection. People who do not share most of what we believe need to be approached differently, and Paul provides us with a good model for doing that.

- *What can you learn from Paul's presentation that can help you with those individuals in your life who believe little of what you do?*

- *Whereas Paul had one major opportunity to speak to the Athenian leaders, most of us have frequent opportunities to speak to the unbelievers in our life. What are some Christian beliefs you can go to that may leave the way open for you to share more down the road?*

Corinth and Home

After leaving Athens, Paul traveled to the city of Corinth (Acts 18:1), which was about forty miles west of Athens. Corinth was "the Las Vegas of its time."[104] The city was "a center for the worship of Aphrodite, the goddess of love, who promoted immorality in the name of religion."[105] The city was so licentious that it generated the term "to corinthianize" (in Greek, *korinthiazomai*), which became a label for sexual debauchery.[106]

Corinth was also a hub of commerce and shipping. It had two working harbors. The western one connected the city "with the central and western Mediterranean," while the eastern one linked the city to "the Aegean Sea and through it with the Black Sea and the eastern Mediterranean." The harbors were linked by "a railroad of wooden logs, three and a half miles in length." This railroad was "laid from west to east across the Isthmus so that ships might be dragged on it from the one harbour to the other."[107]

Corinth was also a Roman colony, which meant that all its citizens were Romans. Of course, not everyone who lived and worked there was a citizen, but everyone benefited from the city's Roman status. The city also served as the capital of the province of Achaia.

The population of Corinth at this time was about two hundred thousand, considerably larger than Athens. That population size made Corinth one of the larger cities in the ancient world.

Finally, Corinth had the honor to host and preside over the Isthmian Games. All the other Greek cities participated in these Olympic-like games. They were held every two years, and "at them the sea-god Poseidon was specially honoured. Corinth paid respect, as Paul put it, to 'many "gods" and many "lords"' (1 Corinthians 8:5)."[108]

Paul came into this large, immoral, idolatrous, bustling city alone. His other traveling companions had not caught up with him yet.

- *Read 1 Corinthians 2:1–5, where Paul relates his personal state when he initially arrived in Corinth. Jot down what stands out to you of the humanity and dedication of this man.*

- *Whom did Paul meet in Corinth, and what did Paul find in common with them (Acts 18:1–3)?*

- *What activity did Paul engage in that was typical for him? Who finally joined him (vv. 4–5)?*

- *How did some people who heard him react to him and his message? What was Paul's response to them (v. 6)?*

- *Luke names two of the individuals who responded in faith to what Paul had presented. Who were they? How did their circle of influence respond to Paul's message (vv. 7–8)?*

- *God came to Paul in a vision. What did God tell his faithful missionary, and what did that lead Paul to do (vv. 9–11)?*

- *As you might imagine, Paul's lengthy stay in Corinth generated some trouble for him. Who led the charge against him? Of what did they accuse him and before whom (vv. 12–13)?*

- *How did this attempt to silence Paul turn out (vv. 14–17)?*

- *After Paul left Corinth, where did he go, and who went with him (vv. 18–19)?*

Paul wrapped up his second missionary journey with a brief stay in Ephesus, where he received a warm reception in the synagogue. Determined not to stay long there, he left for Caesarea and then traveled on to Jerusalem and finally back to Syrian Antioch. The trip from Jerusalem to Antioch was about 335 miles, a three-week journey on foot.

Paul must have been exhausted, for this missionary journey had taken about two-and-a-half years, from April 50 to September 52.[109] And he had encountered a good deal of opposition as well as witnessing numerous conversions to Christ. Paul had evangelized and discipled, and he had defended the faith as well as himself. While customarily beginning ministry in the synagogues wherever he went, he always ended up speaking with gentiles, whether they were Roman citizens or not. The gospel was given to all, and those who responded to it by faith received new life in Jesus Christ—a life empowered by the Holy Spirit.

The Lord effectively worked through Paul and his travel companions, and more was still to come.

Talking It Out

1. When Paul went into synagogues to talk with Jews, he always presented his case for Jesus from God's Word, which for the Jews consisted of what we refer to as the Old Testament. Why do you think Paul always went to Scripture with this audience?

2. Paul didn't go to Scripture at all when he spoke to the Athenians. Instead, he started with their religious devotion and their idols. Why do you think he avoided using Scripture? What would be some of the advantages of not going to the Bible right away with some people?

Paul's Third Missionary Journey

(18:23–21:17)

Luke is not specific regarding how much time in Syrian Antioch Paul spent resting and fellowshipping with believers after his long second missionary journey (Acts 18:23). But Paul didn't stay at his home base and retire. Instead, he launched out again on his third missionary journey, which began in the spring of 53 and went to May of 57.[110] This one took him to "Galatia and Phrygia in central Turkey" (v. 23) and finally to Ephesus (19:1), which is where he spent the bulk of his time. Before arriving in Ephesus, "he encouraged and strengthened the believers" wherever he went (18:23). His journey from Syrian Antioch to Ephesus was about fifteen hundred miles by land. It was likely the same route he had traveled during his second missionary journey with Silas.[111]

Apollos and His Ministry

Before Paul arrived in Ephesus, Luke introduces us to the arrival of another man named Apollos. He, too, was a Jew, and he was a believer in Jesus.

- *Read Acts 18:24–26. What more do you learn about this defender of the faith?*

- *What did Priscilla and Aquila do for him (v. 26)?*

- *Apollos then traveled to the "province of Achaia" (v. 27). What did he bring with him, and what was his ministry in that region (vv. 27–28)?*

Ephesus

While Apollos was serving in Corinth, Paul "arrived in Ephesus" (19:1). This, of course, was the second time Paul had been in Ephesus, but his first stay had been just a brief visit.

- *Read note 'd' for Acts 18:19 and write down key facts you learn there about the city of Ephesus.*

• What is your impression of this city? What kind of issues might Paul face in such a metropolis?

• Whom did Paul initially come across in Ephesus, and what did he do for them (19:1–7)?

• During this three-month ministry activity, where and whom did Paul engage, and how did he do it? Why did some disbelieve, and why did Paul leave with the believers (vv. 8–9)?

- *For more than two years, where did Paul establish his ministry activity, and how far did his teaching spread (v. 10; see also the study notes on this verse)?*

- *How did God work miracles through Paul (vv. 11–12)?*

- *What strange event led to revival in Ephesus, and what else happened as a result (vv. 13–20)?*

- *While still in Ephesus, what plan did Paul initiate (vv. 21–22)?*

ᚺ WORD WEALTH

In the Greek text, the TPT wording "Paul had it in his heart" more literally reads "Paul purposed in the spirit" (v. 21). The Greek word for "purposed" is in the middle voice, which indicates that "Paul's own resolve plays a role in the decision."[112] This is what the TPT wording emphasizes here. The Greek term for "spirit" here is ambiguous; it could refer to Paul's spirit or to the Holy Spirit. In verse 22, where Paul said, "I have to go to Rome also," the words translated "have to" come from the Greek verb *dei* ("must"), "which in Luke's writings usually connotes the divine will."[113] Putting all this together, verses 21–22 reveal that there was a combination of wills at work in Paul's planning. Paul's will and God's will had become in sync. As Bock suggests, "It appears that Paul has a resolve that he lays before God to see if it is from the Spirit."[114] Determining that it was, Paul followed the Spirit's lead, which also linked up with his own longing (cf. Romans 15:22–24).

- *An Ephesian businessman named Demetrius raised alarm over Paul and his teachings. What did he do and say (Acts 19:23–27; revisit note 'd' for 18:19 to regain background for the significance of Demetrius' concern)?*

- *Read 19:28–35 and describe the chaos that followed Demetrius' rallying cry.*

- *How was Paul protected during this outbreak (v. 30)?*

- *Who brought an end to the rioting, and how did he do it (vv. 35–41)?*

- *What did Paul do after this (20:1)?*

Macedonia to Jerusalem

Paul had spent three years in Ephesus (20:31). Now the church there was strong enough for him to move on as he had planned.

Paul's return trip from Macedonia to Jerusalem is summarized by Luke through six travel reports that alternate with five more detailed scenes of ministry activity[115]:

20:1–6	Travel report: Ephesus – Macedonia – Greece – Macedonia – Philippi – Troas
20:7–12	*Ministry: Meeting with believers in Troas*
20:13–17	Travel report: Troas – Assos – Chios – Samos – Miletus
20:18–38	*Ministry: Meeting with the Ephesian elders in Miletus*
21:1–3	Travel report: Miletus – Kos – Patara – Tyre
21:4–6	*Ministry: Meeting with believers in Tyre*
21:7	Travel report: Tyre – Akko
21:7	*Ministry: Meeting with believers in Akko*
21:8	Travel report: Akko – Caesarea
21:8–14	*Ministry: Meeting with believers in Caesarea*
21:15–17	Travel report: Caesarea – Jerusalem

Keeping in mind the charted itinerary, we're going to focus on the five ministry activities.

From Macedonia to Troas

- *How did Paul use his time in Macedonia (20:2)?*

- *What led him to change his plans in Greece (vv. 2–3)?*

- *Notice the use again of the first-person plural in verse 5 ("us"). What does that indicate about who was traveling with Paul at this time?*

- *In verses 7–12, Luke provides details about a Sunday gathering to listen to Paul preach and teach. What terrifying event happened while Paul preached? How were the believers feeling when it was over?*

From Troas to Miletus

- *Why did Paul choose not to revisit Ephesus? What did he choose to do instead (vv. 16–17)?*

- *With the church elders from Ephesus gathered in Miletus to meet with Paul, what did the apostle relate to them (vv. 18–35)? Bullet the main points below.*

- *What did Paul link the Holy Spirit to (v. 28)?*

- *Luke describes in verses 36–38 how Paul and the Ephesian elders parted company. What does his description tell you about Paul's relationship with these elders?*

From Miletus to Tyre

- *In Tyre, how long did Paul and his companions stay, and what happened during his time with fellow Christians there (21:4–6)?*

From Tyre to Caesarea

After spending a day with believers in Akko, Paul and his companions traveled to Caesarea.

- *With whom did they stay in Caesarea (vv. 8–9; also see note 'e' for verse 8)?*

- *A prophet from Judea visited them in Caesarea. Who was he, and what did he prophesy while with Paul and his companions? What impact did his words and actions have on the other believers there (vv. 10–14)?*

From Caesarea to Jerusalem

- *Paul picked up more companions on his way to Jerusalem. Who were they (v. 15–16)?*

- *Who was Mnason (v. 16; also see note 'i' for this verse)?*

- *When Paul and his party arrived in Jerusalem, how were they received (v. 17)?*

In Luke's account, this marks the end of Paul's missionary journeys, but the close of Acts is yet to come. The apostle Paul and the Christian faith are going to be put on trial all the way to the capital city of the Roman Empire, its central hub—Rome. And through it all, the gospel will continue to spread, the church will be strengthened even more, and Christ will be exalted ever higher.

◆ EXPERIENCE GOD'S HEART

- *Paul could not have traveled and ministered and endured all he did without also having a vibrant relationship with Jesus Christ. He knew the Lord, he followed the Lord's lead, and he accomplished the Lord's will for his life. How is your heart toward God? Do you trust him and seek him and follow him? Do you stand up for him? Are you willing to sacrifice anything for him? Prayerfully reflect on your own spiritual condition before God. He loves you as you are, and yet he loves you so much that he won't leave you as you are. He wants you to grow, to mature, to become strong, to persevere, to not lose hope but to grow more and more trusting in him. Are you cooperating with him in all of this? Go to him. Spend time in his presence. Rest in him. Wait on him. And do this regularly. He upholds the humble.*

9 SHARE GOD'S HEART

- *No one should do the Christian life alone. Paul didn't. He had travel companions, and he met with fellow believers just about everywhere he went. We need one another. Are you meeting with fellow believers? Are you doing it enough to feed your own soul as well as to help nourish others in the faith? Even if you are not connected with a congregation right now, find other Christians with whom you can meet. Share your experiences, share what you are learning from God's Word, pray together, work together when you can, minister to others. Christ is meant to be shared. Give. Give even more than you receive, and you will be living a Christlike life.*

Talking It Out

1. Most of us live in a culture used to immediate results. Paul, however, spent three years in Ephesus, evangelizing and discipling and building up the fledgling church even in the face of occasional opposition. Discuss what it takes to build something new even when "God is the one who brings the supernatural growth" (1 Corinthians 3:7).

2. Christianity makes exclusivist claims: for example, there is one God, not many; Jesus is the Son of God, and there is no other; the way to salvation is through Christ alone; all human beings are sinners in need of repentance with one sole exception—Jesus. Such claims are true, trustworthy, and deserve our full acceptance. But when we make that commitment, we thereby say no to so much else. Demetris in Ephesus grasped this, which is why he saw his livelihood threatened—a livelihood steeped in the business of idolatry (Acts 19:23–27). What businesses today are threatened by serious commitments to Christ? And if some are not that should be, what might that say about Christian commitment today?

LESSON 10

Captivity in Jerusalem

(21:18–23:32)

Have you ever been falsely accused? If so, did the charge come from a fellow employee, an employer, a teacher, a church leader, or someone else? Did the accusation have any semblance of truth, or was it so far off that you found it hard to imagine how anyone could have leveled it against you? How did you deal with it? What was the fallout?

When the apostle Paul and his fellow missionaries arrived in Jerusalem, which was then the center of Judaism, he found that he had become the subject of a "rumor" that contained false claims about him. And these claims, if true, would do more than discourage Jews from listening to his message. If the allegations were true, the Jews would brand him as an apostate worthy of death. Paul was looking at a serious threat to his ministry and to his life.

Trouble in Jerusalem

After Paul provided Jacob and the Jerusalem Christian elders with a detailed report of his third missionary journey and received their praise (Acts 21:18–20), these church leaders gave Paul some troubling news.

- *What was that news, and how far had it spread (vv. 20–21)?*

🐾 DIGGING DEEPER

The charges embedded in the rumor were three. First, Paul was supposedly telling Jews to "abandon Moses" (v. 21). If true, then Paul would have been inciting the Jews to stop keeping the commandments of the law and thereby become gentiles. This would have made Paul a seducer of the people, someone who tried to move Jews to apostatize from Judaism, an act that would make him subject to capital punishment (Deuteronomy 13:12–18).

The second charge was that Paul was teaching Jews that "they don't need to circumcise their children" (Acts 21:21). Circumcision was one of the Mosaic law's central commands, and it was a "defining mark of God's covenant with Israel."[116] Was Paul really saying that Jewish male children did not have to bear this mark of God's covenant with his chosen people?

The third charge was that Paul instructed Jews to stop heeding "Jewish customs." In other words, Paul allegedly taught that Jews should not keep the Mosaic laws that had to do with how they were to live on a daily basis.

If all these charges were true, then Paul would have been teaching Jews to completely change their identity and their practices—to reject all that the Torah taught them. Was that Paul's teaching?

Well, the charges blurred distinctions that Paul had made. We don't have the space to go into these in detail, but we need to provide some information so you can better assess where Paul really stood on these matters.

Starting with the first charge, Paul did not teach Jews to abandon Moses and the Torah and become gentiles. Rather, he treasured Jewish history and writings and the fulfillment of their prophecies in the God-man, Jesus. And he believed and taught that God still had a magnificent future for Israel (Romans 9–11). Paul also still saw great value in the Mosaic law. What he denied, however, was that the law could save. That was never the law's function or purpose. We are saved by faith in God's Messiah, Jesus, the one who fulfilled the law's requirements (Galatians 2:15–21). Jews could still live as Jews and comply with the Mosaic law, but they must do so realizing that they will not find salvation in it.

Gentiles, on the other hand, didn't need to become Jews before they became Christians. As long as they complied with the Jerusalem council's decision as laid out in Acts 15, they were to live according to Christ. They did not need to practice the Jewish sacrifices, become circumcised, or do anything else that was distinctively Jewish.

Regarding the second charge, there is no evidence that Paul instructed Jews not to circumcise their male children. While Paul taught that circumcision didn't matter (1 Corinthians 7:17–20; Galatians 6:15–16), he never forbade its practice.

As far as the third charge was concerned, Paul did teach that believers were free from keeping the law, but he never told Jews that they could not follow it. In fact, in his evangelism efforts, he said that he "became Jewish to the Jewish people in order to win them to the Messiah" (1 Corinthians 9:20). While free from the Mosaic law, he followed the law among Jews in order to win them to Christ. What he taught is that "The law was our guardian until Christ came so that we would be saved by faith. But now that faith has come we are no longer under the guardian of the law. You have all become true children of God by faith in Jesus Christ" (Galatians 3:24–26). As important as the law was and is, through Christ it has fulfilled its purpose. The issue is not whether we should keep the law. The issue is whether we should entrust ourselves to the one whom the law prophesied would come. And the answer is yes!

The Messiah Jesus has fulfilled the law and thereby freed us from having to keep it. Now we have his righteousness—a righteousness we could never attain by law-keeping.

In short, Jews could keep their Jewishness as long as they didn't force that on gentiles and didn't assume that law-keeping—as futile as that was—could earn them God's salvific favor. Salvation didn't come by law but by grace.

- *In an attempt to undermine the charges against him, the Jerusalem church leaders urged Paul to do something publicly. What was it (Acts 21:23–24)?*

- *What did the church leaders say about gentile (non-Jewish) believers? Did they ask Paul to do anything for that group (v. 25)?*

- *Did Paul follow their direction (v. 26)?*

DIGGING DEEPER

Luke doesn't specify what vow the four men took or why it would require them to shave their heads. Bible scholars have provided various suggestions, but the one that seems to fit best is that these men had become ceremonially unclean and needed to cleanse themselves in keeping with their Nazarite vows (Numbers 6:1–12). Paul, however, was not a Nazarite, but it was customary for Jews to purify themselves due to defilement from traveling in gentile areas. So while Paul (as well as the other church leaders, including the apostles) did not believe that their association with gentiles made them unclean (Acts 10–11), Paul was willing to curb his freedom in Christ for the sake of the sensitivities of traditionally minded Jews. Schnabel points out other reasons why the church leaders may have suggested that Paul go through a purification ritual:

> Any Jew who visited the temple in order
> to offer sacrifices and partake of hallowed
> foodstuffs had to immerse himself in
> water so as not to defile, through mere
> physical contact, any of the consecrated
> vessels, clothing, or foodstuffs. Persons
> defiled by ritual impurities such as eating
> or drinking ritually impure foodstuffs or
> liquids, washing or bathing in any bath
> other than a valid *miqweh*, or having any
> form of physical contact with a Gentile, and
> who wanted to enter the inner courts of the
> temple, were deemed completely pure after
> ritual immersion without having to wait
> until sunset.[117]

Whatever the precise rationale for the purification rituals, Paul participated in them and paid the costs for himself and these four men.

- *Despite Paul's actions, some "Jews from western Turkey" (Acts 21:27) turned other Jews against him. What did they do and claim (vv. 27–29)?*

Bringing a gentile past the outer temple court where gentiles were allowed and into any of the inner courts was anathema. Because these Turkish Jews had seen the Ephesian Trophimus with Paul (see 20:4), they had assumed wrongly that Trophimus was with Paul this time. While a gentile entering the inner courts of the temple would not have been a problem for Paul's theology (Romans 14:14), Paul knew that it was a serious matter for his fellow Jews. Inscriptions in Latin and Greek outside of the inner temple courts "prohibited, under penalty of death, non-Jews from accessing the inner courts."[118] Paul would not have violated that prohibition, especially at a time when so many Jews had already believed false accusations against him.

A Riot and a Rescue

- *What, then, occurred in the temple courts (v. 30)?*

- *What was the mob close to doing to Paul, and how was he rescued (vv. 31–32)?*

- *What action did the Roman military commander take with the hostile crowd, and was it effective in ascertaining the truth of the situation (vv. 33–36)?*

- *What did Paul convince the commander to let him do (vv. 37–40)?*

Paul's Defense

Paul stood before the mob that wanted to kill him and offered a defense (*apologia*), and he spoke to them in their own language, which led them to listen to him rather than try to shout him down (22:1–2).

- *First Paul gave the crowd his Jewish credentials (v. 3). What were they?*

- *Then he added evidence of his zealous commitment to the Jewish faith (vv. 4–5). What was that?*

- *Next Paul detailed what happened to him on the way to Damascus and how he became a convert to Jesus (vv. 6–16). Summarize the highlights of this story.*

- *Finally, Paul told about an experience he had in Jerusalem while praying in the temple area (vv. 17–21). Whom did Paul see? What did this person say to Paul? What about this person's revelation to Paul would have provoked the ire of those hearing his defense?*

- *How did the crowd respond to Paul (vv. 22–23)?*

A Roman Interrogation and a Jewish Disruption

A Roman (gentile) military commander would not be expected to understand the complexities of Jewish belief and practice. So while the commander once again rescued Paul from the fierceness of the crowd, he thought it would be prudent to whip and interrogate Paul "to find out what he said that so infuriated the crowd" (v. 24).

- *An exchange then took place between the commander and Paul (vv. 25–30). What did Paul reveal to the commander, and how did this change their plans for punishing Paul?*

- *Brought to a hearing before the Jewish council (the Sanhedrin) in Jerusalem, Paul began his defense (23:1). What did the high priest presiding over the council then do (v. 2)?*

The start of Paul's defense was a declaration of his innocence of the false accusations against him. A Jew who had lived his life doing God's will and had maintained "a perfectly clear conscience" in respect to that life could not be guilty of the charges against him. The high priest's order to strike Paul in the mouth was "an attempt to brand Paul as a liar."[119]

- *Paul's response was quick and sharp (v. 3). What was it?*

Paul viewed the high priest's action as a violation of how a just judge should conduct himself (Leviticus 19:15). But that's not how those near Paul saw it. They interpreted his denunciation of the high priest as an insult (Acts 23:4).

- *With that misinterpretation stated, Paul corrected it (v. 5). What two points did he make?*

Paul's point about not knowing that Ananias was the high priest could just have been a statement of fact, which seems unlikely since he had been in Jerusalem for some time, and he had received some news about Jerusalem during his third missionary journey. It could be that Paul was speaking ironically, in essence saying, *I had no idea that a man who would act so injudiciously was serving as high priest.* If that's the tone Paul took, then his reference to Exodus 22:28 may also have been somewhat ironic, suggesting that the way Ananias behaved demonstrated that he was not really a representative of the people and of God's way, despite the official title he held. This interpretation of his comments fits with the judgment Paul cast on Ananias in Acts 23:3. Whether Paul was speaking ironically or not, he seemed to have concluded from this part of his encounter that he would not get a fair hearing from the members of the Sanhedrin.

- *At this juncture in the interrogation, what did Paul realize, and how did he take advantage of that (v. 6; see also the notes on this verse)?*

- *What were the doctrinal differences between the Sadducees and the Pharisees ("separated ones") regarding Paul's belief in the resurrection, and what level of dispute between the two groups did it create (vv. 7–9)? Who finally sided with Paul?*

- *With the dispute leading to an intense "shouting match," how did the Roman commander intervene (v. 10)?*

- *How did the Lord reassure Paul after such a trying few days (v. 11)?*

A Foiled Plot

The Jewish response to Paul became murderous again.

- *What plot was hatched against Paul and by whom? Who supported them (vv. 12–15)?*

- *Who discovered the plot, and how did the Roman commander learn of it (vv. 16–21)?*

- *What course of action did the commander take, and was it effective in saving Paul (vv. 22–32)?*

Paul had been delivered from death—yet again. It required getting him out of town and even into a different province and city. And he had an incredible military escort to boot! He was safe once again, though still in custody—not as a criminal, for no one had brought formal charges against him yet. He needed to get a fair hearing before a fair judge. Ironically, it would not be a Jewish judge but a gentile one. Would he be fair-minded? Would he listen to this controversial man? That's what we'll find out in the next lesson.

EXPERIENCE GOD'S HEART

What made Paul controversial? Did he try to be adversarial? No. Did he get in people's faces and yell at them? No. Was he condescending? No. What he did, however, was to present and defend the truth about Jesus and the implications of that for belief, behavior, and belonging.

To many Jews, this truth amounted to the abolition of all they held dear, even though that was not what Paul taught.

To many gentiles, Paul's claims seemed foolish, profit-crushing, and dishonoring to the gods they worshiped. Were his claims foolish? Not at all. They were the height of wisdom—divine wisdom, not the speculations of mere human wisdom (1 Corinthians 2). Were they profit-crushing? Yes, if one's livelihood depended on all the trades wrapped around idolatry. Otherwise, not at all. Paul's teaching actually served to redirect the talents of commerce to much more productive endeavors. Were his teachings dishonoring to the gods? No, because Paul knew that the gods did not exist. They were man-made creations and had no independent reality at all (8:4–6; 12:2; cf. Acts 14:15; Romans 1:21–23; 1 Thessalonians 1:9). You can't dishonor what is not real.

So whether the audience was Jewish or gentile, Paul's teaching was often misunderstood, mischaracterized, mishandled, and mistaken for promoting apostasy, heresy, and even rebellion against the Roman state. False charges led to death threats, murderous plots, arrests, imprisonment, beatings, and a marred reputation.

And yet, God was with Paul, working through him, advancing the gospel, delivering people from the penalty and power of sin, and healing their bodies, minds, and hearts. While the truth bred opposition, it also gave birth to the church—the body of Christ, the family of God. And that has grown and become worldwide since its Spirit-announced beginnings in Acts 2.

• *Are you an advocate for the truth? How so?*

- *Have you paid a personal cost for your truth advocacy? If so, what has it been?*

- *Has God been working through you? How do you know? What are the signs of his involvement?*

- *If you have become timid or fearful in advocating for Christian truth, why has this occurred? What have you learned from Acts so far that can help you build your courage?*

♥ SHARE GOD'S HEART

Paul stood up for himself and for his Christian faith. He would also modify his behavior, curbing the expression of his own freedom in Christ, in order to open more opportunities to present the truth of the gospel to those who needed to hear it (1 Corinthians 9:19–23).

- *Have you been willing to restrict your freedom at times so you can open doors for the gospel? If so, describe how you did this.*

- *What opportunities do you now have to share Christ that may require you to dress differently, eat differently, wear your hair differently, go to a place you wouldn't normally go, or do something else that temporarily limits you—all for the sake of the gospel? Are you willing to limit your freedom so you can present the tremendous freedom that others can find in Jesus Christ?*

Talking It Out

1. Discuss the power that accusations have and how we can deflate those allegations that are false and effectively deal with any truth some of them might contain.

2. Sometimes we can accommodate the sensitivities of others without compromising our Christian convictions. Other times, however, we should not. Review what Paul yielded on and what he stood up for. What insight does that provide for fellow Christians concerning what we should defend and what we can bend without compromising the essential truths of the faith?

LESSON 11

Captivity in Caesarea

(23:33–26:32)

When Paul arrived in Caesarea (June 57),[120] his military escort, which at this point consisted of just the seventy horsemen (Acts 23:24, 31–32), presented the letter from Claudius Lysias, the Roman commander, to Felix, who was the Roman governor of the province of Judea at the time.

Earlier in his life, Antonius Felix had been a slave and was freed by the Roman emperor Claudius, who appointed him to the governorship of Judea around AD 53. The Roman historian Tacitus reports that during Felix's time as governor, "he indulged in all kinds of cruelty and lust." Tacitus adds that Felix considered himself "licensed to commit any crime, relying on the influence that he possessed at [the imperial] court." Felix had three wives, one of whom was Drusilla, who was "a daughter of King Herod Agrippa." Before marrying Felix, Drusilla had been wife to Azizus, king of Emesa, and it was "through the influence of Simon, a magician," that Felix got her to consent to marry him.[121] This was the man who would now hear Paul's case. And Felix told Paul that he would give him a hearing after his accusers had arrived. Until then, "he ordered that Paul be kept under guard in Herod's palace" (v. 35).

THE BACKSTORY

King Herod Agrippa II had several palaces in Judea. The one in Caesarea was large, beautiful, highly functional, and expensive to build. The palace was built on piers that extended 330 feet offshore. It had frescoed rooms and a fresh-water pool "adorned with a statue in the middle." An upper part of the palace has been identified as the Praetorium, which "was the administrative wing of the palace and likely included quarters for the Praetorian Guard as well as holding cells for prisoners." It's likely that this was "the location of the trials of Paul before Festus and Agrippa II (Acts 25:1–26:32). From the Praetorium, Paul would have had constant view of the comings and goings of the harbor, with a persistent tug on his heart to travel to Rome."[122]

Before Felix

- *Who arrived in Caesarea to "present formal charges" against the apostle Paul (Acts 24:1)?*

- *Read through Tertullus' presentation before the governor Felix and summarize the charges he made against Paul (vv. 2–8).*

- *Do you think his charges were true? Did they accurately depict what you have read so far about Paul's actions? Explain your answer.*

- *After the other Jews present voiced their agreement with Tertullus' case (v. 9), Felix gave Paul the floor to answer his accusers (v. 10). Review Paul's defense (vv. 10–21). What were his answers to the charges against him?*

- *Do you think that Paul effectively rebutted the charges? Why or why not?*

• Felix then drew the session to a close, declaring what his next step would be, which was what (v. 22)?

• What order did Felix make about Paul (v. 23)? Do you think this would have pleased Paul's accusers?

• What happened next shows that Felix never did render a decisive judgment on Paul's case. Read verses 24–27. What do you think Felix's actions, the length of his procrastination, and his final disposition toward Paul reveal about Felix's motives?

DIGGING DEEPER

The Roman emperor Nero (AD 54–68) recalled Felix in the year 59 due to serious allegations that were leveled against him. As Schnabel explains, the "leaders of the Jewish community in Caesarea went to Rome" and accused Felix of "maladministration." Continuing, Schnabel writes:

> This followed an incident in Caesarea where the Jews had claimed that Caesarea belonged to them, while the Greeks used the (pagan) temples that Herod had erected as proof that Caesarea was not a Jewish city. Felix ended the ensuing riots in the agora by sending in his troops, who killed many Jews, and Felix subsequently plundered their property. Both the Jewish and Greek communities of Caesarea sent their leaders to Rome [to present their case against what Felix had done]. Felix was spared serious punishment by the emperor Nero only because Felix's influential brother Pallas pleaded for him...Felix was replaced by Porcius Festus, who was governor from AD 59–62.[123]

Before Festus

Porcius Festus arrived as Felix's replacement as governor of Judea. According to Josephus, Festus was a welcome contrast to Felix as well as to Albinus, the man who eventually succeeded him. Apparently Albinus was just as corrupt as Felix had been. Festus walked into a load of trouble that Felix had failed to handle and even partially created through his poor ability to manage Judea. "There was a shocking breakdown of law and order in the countryside, and open armed hostility between the rival factions in the [political and civil] hierarchy...Festus knew that he could not afford to alienate or offend any collaborating elements in the Jewish population."[124]

- *What was among Festus' first acts of business soon after arriving in Judea (Acts 25:1–5)?*

- *Soon after he returned to Caesarea, what did Festus do regarding Paul and his accusers (vv. 6–7)? Were Paul's accusers able to provide sufficient evidence to make their charges stick?*

- *What was Paul's defense against the charges (v. 8)? Since the prosecution could not make their case, did Paul need to say anything more than he did?*

- *Festus made a counterproposal to Paul. What was it (v. 9)?*

- *Knowing he would not get a fair trial in Jerusalem with the Sanhedrin sitting in judgment, to whom did Paul appeal for judgment (vv. 10–11)? What did Festus then do (v. 12)?*

# THE BACKSTORY

As a Roman citizen, Paul had the right to appeal his case to the Roman emperor. Roman law protected Roman citizens "from violent coercion and capital trials by provincial administrators."[125] Paul knew his life was at stake. He also knew that God wanted him in Rome. Appealing his case to the emperor accomplished both objectives: protecting his life and fulfilling the divine prerogative.

At this time in Roman history, the emperor was Nero, a ruler who, in AD 64, would launch a horrific persecution against Christians. But when Paul made his appeal, which was likely in late 59,[126] Nero's reign had not gone off the rails yet. The early years of his rule (54–62) "were looked upon as something of a Golden Age."[127] Nero was still listening to his tutor, Seneca, a Stoic philosopher, and to the prefect of the praetorian guard, Afranius Burrus. Paul had a chance with Nero to gain a fair hearing, so he took it.

Before Festus and Agrippa

- *Who showed up in Caesarea the following day, and whom did they meet with (v. 23; see the TPT note on this verse)?*

- *What did Festus say about Paul when introducing him to his guests (vv. 24–27)? What trouble was Festus having with the prospect of sending Paul off to Rome?*

Festus could not find a justifiable charge against Paul that the emperor could rule on. Religious disputes that did not significantly violate a governor's ability to keep the peace were typically left for the religious parties to work out themselves. Paul's accusers were Jewish, and their charges against him were largely religious in nature. A pagan Roman governor could not adjudicate such a dispute; Festus likely didn't even understand the religious issues at stake.

Festus looked to King Herod Agrippa II and his sister Bernice to help him figure out what to say about Paul when he sent him off to Rome. Roman officials often consulted Agrippa II on religious matters because he controlled the temple treasury in Jerusalem and the vestments of the high priest, which gave him the authority to appoint high priests.[128]

- *Agrippa II gave Paul permission to make his defense before him (Acts 26:1). As Paul began, what signs of deference did he make toward the king (vv. 2–3)?*

- *What did Paul say about his life as a faithful Jew (vv. 4–5)?*

- *For what reason did Paul say that he was now on trial (vv. 6–7)?*

- *What did Paul relate about his former opposition to Jesus-followers that further credentialed him as a zealot Jew (vv. 8–12)?*

- *Summarize what Paul said about the revelation that he received while still hostile to followers of Christ (vv. 13–18).*

- *Did Paul believe that he had been faithful to the revelation, and did he think that this was why his life had been threatened (vv. 19–21)? Support your answer.*

- *What, then, had been the substance of his teaching (vv. 22–23)? Did he view his teaching as undermining or fulfilling what Scripture teaches?*

- *At the end of Paul's speech, what did Festus conclude about him? How did Paul respond (vv. 24–25)?*

- *Paul then turned his attention to King Agrippa II. What did Paul remind him about the prophets, and what surprising statement did Agrippa make (vv. 26–29)?*

- *What conclusions did the governing officials draw after hearing Paul's defense (vv. 30–32)?*

- *What are your conclusions about Paul and his defense? How effective of an apologist (defender) was he?*

 EXPERIENCE GOD'S HEART

On countless occasions, the apostle Paul and the other apostles not only presented the good news about Jesus Christ but also defended it against criticisms and accusations. When needed, they also defended their own actions. Paul described this part of the Christian mission this way:

> Although we live in the natural realm, we
> don't wage a military campaign employing
> human weapons, using manipulation to
> achieve our aims. Instead, our spiritual
> weapons are energized with divine power
> to effectively dismantle the defenses
> behind which people hide. We can

demolish every deceptive fantasy that
opposes God and break through every
arrogant attitude that is raised up in
defiance of the true knowledge of God.
We capture, like prisoners of war, every
thought and insist that it bow in obedience
to the Anointed One. (2 Corinthians 10:3–5)

The apostle Peter made it clear that such a mission is for every Christian to at least prepare for: "If anyone asks about the hope living within you, always be ready to explain [that is, defend, *apologia*] your faith with gentleness and respect" (1 Peter 3:15–16).

Are you prepared to offer a defense of the Christian faith? Your ability to do this will not only help others who need to hear the evidence for the faith, but it can also answer questions and doubts you may have. You can learn much about Christian apologetics and how to offer a defense by reading at least two books. One is by the highly respected New Testament scholar F. F. Bruce, entitled *The Defense of the Gospel in the New Testament*. He first explains what the gospel is and how Jesus presented it. Then he explains how the gospel confronted the Jews, pagans, the Roman empire, and even attempts to deviate from it. Throughout the book, he shows how Jesus and the apostles defended the gospel before its critics.

The other book, *The Apologetics of Jesus*, is by renowned Christian apologist and theologian Norman L. Geisler and researcher and apologist Patrick Zukeran. These authors zero in on the many ways Jesus used a host of tools to defend his person and message—tools including testimony, discourse, reason, parables, prophecy, miracles, and his resurrection. They provide insight into Jesus' apologetic method and the Holy Spirit's role in this part of Jesus' ministry.

Between these two resources, you will receive a good deal of help in learning how Jesus and his followers defended the faith and how you can apply what they did to your life situation. (For a handful of apologetic resources dealing with contemporary objections to the Christian faith as well as providing evidence showing that Christians have good reasons to believe, go to the endnote provided at the end of this sentence.[129])

❤ SHARE GOD'S HEART

How we share our faith in Christ is every bit as important as the evidence we provide. Three resources have proven themselves to be especially beneficial in this regard. The first, now a classic, is *Out of the Saltshaker and into the World: Evangelism as a Way of Life*, by Rebecca Manley Pippert, a national consultant on evangelism. First published in 1979 and issued in a new edition in 2021, this book has sold nearly a million copies and inspired countless more to present the gospel and live it out in ways that will draw people closer to Christ.

A second resource is *Tactics: A Game Plan for Discussing Your Christian Convictions*, by Gregory Koukl, the founder and president of Stand to Reason. As the back cover copy on the book says, "*Tactics* teaches you how to maneuver comfortably and graciously as you share your faith with others." *Tactics* is especially helpful for learning how to navigate minefields in conversations, stop challengers in their tracks, turn the tables on objectors, and get people thinking about Jesus.

The third book is titled *Conversational Evangelism: Connecting with People to Share Jesus*, written by David Geisler with his father, Norman Geisler. Both men established and grew Norm Geisler International Ministries, where apologetics, evangelism, and discipleship are interwoven in such a way that believers can learn how to seamlessly engage in these spiritual disciplines as they walk with Christ in a troubled world. In their book *Conversational Evangelism*, they focus their efforts on evangelism without ignoring the interplay between apologetics and discipleship.

Talking It Out

1. Paul made it clear to the Roman governor Festus and King Herod Agrippa II that he desired for both of them to become followers of Jesus (Acts 26:29). Paul also urged believers to pray for political leaders, for the Lord "longs for everyone to embrace his life and return to the full knowledge of the truth" (1 Timothy 2:2–4). Take time now to pray for your political leaders. No matter their party, positions, or policies, every human being needs Christ.

2. Paul spoke about how Jesus revealed himself to the one who was persecuting him and arresting, imprisoning, and serving up for execution those who were following him. Paul came to faith in Jesus. If someone with his background and hostility toward Christ could come to embrace him by faith, anyone can. Of course, just because a person can come to Christ does not mean that he or she will. Still, we can pray for such individuals and, when the opportunity arises, speak to them about Jesus too. Whom can you pray for? Whom can you speak to? And if, for whatever reason, you are not the person to share the faith with someone who needs Christ, you can still pray that God will open the way for another believer to link up with this needy person. Compose a list of people you can pray for. Prepare to speak to those you can. Then look for those opportunities that God opens and avail yourself of them.

LESSON 12

Captivity in Rome

(27:1–28:31)

Paul had appealed to Caesar, and to Caesar he would be sent. Festus would honor Paul's right as a Roman citizen. But the trip to Rome was a long one,[130] and various perils plagued it, especially due to changes in weather. While Paul would eventually arrive in the capital city of the empire, his life was imperiled more than once, yet God demonstrated his sovereignty over the trip and his favor for Paul and his companions.

Sea Voyage to Italy

- *For the sea voyage to Italy, Paul brought with him two companions. One is indicated by the use of "we," and the other was from Macedonia. Who were they (Acts 27:1–2)?*

- *The Roman governor Festus called for the voyage. Whom did he put in charge of Paul and the "other prisoners" (v. 1)?*

According to New Testament scholar Richard Longenecker, the soldiers under Julius' charge were a "special body of imperial guards" called *speculatores*. They were "assigned to various police and judicial functions."[131] So Paul and the prisoners with him had a Roman guard escort to look after them while the ship's captain and crew took care of the ship.

Luke likely gained passage as Paul's personal physician, while Aristarchus may have gone aboard as Paul's servant or assistant. We know from the "we" passages that Luke remained with Paul all the way to Rome (see 27:1–9, 16, 18, 20, 27, 29; 28:1–2, 7, 10–16). Aristarchus completed the voyage as well, and he, along with Luke, remained with Paul during his imprisonment in Rome (Colossians 4:10; Philemon 24).

Ports, Ships, and Dangerous Weather

While Luke doesn't mention it, they must have embarked from the city of Caesarea, where Festus resided and had heard Paul's case. The ship came "from the port of Adramyttium" (Acts 27:2). The city of Adramyttium was "a seaport of Mysia on the northwest coast of Asia Minor, opposite the island of Lesbos."[132] The plan was "to stop at various ports along the coast of southwestern Turkey" (v. 2).

- *Read verses 3–9. At which four places did the ship dock after leaving Caesarea? What happened at the first two ports?*

- *What weather issues did the vessel face, and what did the crew have to do to try to counter them?*

- *What occurred at Fair Havens (vv. 9–12)? What was Paul's advice? Did the officer in charge heed his advice? If not, why?*

 THE BACKSTORY

Sidon, the first port after Caesarea, was "an ancient Phoenician port some seventy miles north of Caesarea and twenty-five miles north of Tyre."[133] Due to "its glass and purple industry and to the significance of its harbor,"[134] Sidon was a wealthy city. The fact that Paul was allowed to leave the ship and visit friends in the area speaks to the trust that the commander Julius had in him. Though Luke doesn't mention this, since Paul was one of the prisoners, his leave from the ship was likely with the accompaniment of one of the Roman guards.

The second port, Myra, "was the most illustrious city in Lycia, with distinguished public buildings, a very large theater, and many evidences of wealth...Its port became the natural port of call for grain ships bound for Rome from Egypt."[135]

Knidus was the third port, and it was "the last port of call before sailing west across the Aegean for the Greek mainland."[136] But because of strong northerly winds, Paul's ship was blown off course, so the ship's captain sailed along "the southern coast ('the lee') of Crete, the 160-mile-long island southeast of Greece. Passing Cape Salome on the eastern tip of Crete, the ship entered the small bay of Fair Havens."[137] But the bay was not suitable for the large grain ship to remain there through the winter (Acts 27:12). A larger and safer port was just forty miles west of Fair Havens. Called Phineka, this port would protect the ship from the harsh northern gales that blew during the winter months. The problem was that to get to Phineka from Fair Havens, the ship would be exposed to those northern winds for much of the journey. Still, the hope was that the ship could make it, though it would be a struggle.

Surviving a Northeaster—Barely

- *What gave the ship's crew hope that they would make it to Phineka (v. 13)?*

- *What dashed that hope (vv. 14–15)?*

- *What steps did the crew take to save themselves and their ship (vv. 16–19)?*

- *Were these measures enough to salvage their hope? What added to their despair (v. 20)?*

- *What solace did Paul provide for the ship's crew and passengers (vv. 21–26)?*

- *What indications did the crew have that they were getting closer to land (vv. 27–28)?*

• *What tragedy did Paul prevent from happening (vv. 29–32)?*

• *Paul then urged everyone on board to eat. Why did he do this? How many people were fed? What did this do for morale (vv. 33–37)? What did the crew then do to further lighten the ship's load (v. 38)?*

• *Read about the end of this ordeal in verses 39–44. Summarize the key events, including what almost happened to Paul and the other prisoners. Did everyone survive the shipwreck as Paul had predicted?*

Recovery on Malta

With all the crew, guards, and passengers alive, they found themselves on the island of Malta in the Mediterranean Sea (Acts 28:1). Malta is about "18 miles long and 8 miles wide. It lies 58 miles south of Sicily and 180 miles north and east of the African coast...In Paul's day the island was known for its prosperity and residential architecture, and its native population must have spoken not only Phoenician but also some Latin and Greek."[138] The ship likely came to ground on the east coast of Malta. The island was first named by the Phoenicians. They called it *melita*, which means "a place of refuge," which it was for Paul and the rest of those who survived the great storm and the shipwreck.

- *How did the natives of the island welcome Paul and the other survivors (28:2)?*

- *What happened to Paul that led the islanders to think that he was a god (vv. 3–6)?*

Longenecker comments: "Luke gives us such a vividly detailed account of the [snake] incident because he wants his readers to appreciate that Paul was not only a heaven-directed man with a God-given message but also a heaven-protected man. The powerful account of the storm and shipwreck has shown this, and now this vignette stresses it once more."[139]

- *In verses 7–10, Luke wraps up the story of the survivors' stay in Malta with an account of what happened at the house of Publius, the island's Roman governor. What miracle did Paul perform for Publius, and how did the islanders respond?*

Back to Sea

- *"After three months" on Malta, how did the ship's survivors continue their journey, and where did they travel (vv. 11–14)?*

- *Puteoli was one of the principal ports of southern Italy. After arriving there, whom did they meet, and for how long did they remain (v. 14)? What does this say about how Paul was regarded by the Roman commander Julius?*

- *As Paul, Luke, and Aristarchus were still on the road to the great city of Rome, accompanied by the imperial guard, who came out to greet them, and where did they meet them (v. 15; see the notes on this verse)? What do these greeting parties and the distance they traveled reveal about how they regarded Paul and his companions?*

 # DIGGING DEEPER

When Luke informs us about believers going out to meet Paul, he doesn't tell us anything about the church at Rome, including when it began. The fact is that no one really knows with certainty the origin of this church. As Bruce states:

It is impossible to be sure when Christianity was first brought to Rome. Priscilla and Aquila, who were among the Jews expelled from Rome by the Emperor Claudius in AD 49, met Paul in Corinth [the] next year and became his firm and lifelong friends. Yet he never speaks of them as though they were converts of his, and the probability is that they were members of the primitive Christian community in Rome before they were forced to leave the city.[140]

The Roman historian Suetonius states that the emperor Claudius expelled Jews from the capital because they "caused continuous disturbances at the instigation of Chrestus."[141] "Chrestus" was a variant spelling of "Christ." Luke mentions this expulsion when he introduces Priscilla and Aquila (Acts 18:2), who had arrived in Corinth after leaving Rome.

This expulsion of Jews from the city could have affected many thousands of people. At this time, "almost as many Jews lived in Rome as normally lived in Jerusalem." Bruce reports that "six Jewish catacombs or underground burial areas have been discovered around Rome, and from inscriptions in these we know the names of eleven Roman synagogues."[142]

Along with this Jewish population in Rome, we know that by the time Paul wrote his letter to the church at Rome (likely around AD 56), the church was already well established, and its "testimony" was "spreading throughout the world" (Romans 1:8). In fact, as Bruce states, the Roman church "may well have been one of the earliest churches to be founded outside Palestine, and we have seen ground for believing that ten years before Paul's arrival the advance of the gospel in the Jewish community at Rome led to riots which brought imperial displeasure upon the community" (Acts 18:2).[143]

So Paul had come into a city with a Jewish population that had partially returned once Claudius' edict had been rescinded and with a Christian community still proselytizing to Jew and gentile alike.

Prisoner in Rome

The city of Rome in Paul's day was the long-time seat of political and administrative power in the Roman Empire. Rome was a sprawling city built on and around seven hills. The city grew up around the Tiber River, which "emptied into the Mediterranean about twenty miles (32 km) downriver from Rome at the port of Ostia, giving the city fairly ready access to sea trade."[144] An extensive road system throughout the empire led travelers not only from one city to another but also to Rome itself, guaranteeing that the capital would enjoy abundant trade by land, not just by sea. The city's population was over a million. The second largest city in the empire—Alexandria, Egypt—had just three hundred thousand. The language of government and law was Latin, while Greek was the primary language of business and trade. The city boasted a large Greek library and an expansive Roman one.

The famous Colosseum had not yet been built when Paul arrived in the city around AD 62, but the Forum was already there. The Forum glistened "with marble, bronze, and gold." It had beautiful statues, proud columns, and stately arches. A "small circular temple of Vesta"—the "goddess of the hearth fire"—was at the Forum, as was an altar to Hercules, "worshipped as a god of victory and also as a god of commercial enterprise."[145] The Forum also included the house of the Roman senate. It was at the Forum that "the politics and piety of the city blended together to proclaim that Rome's power was the result of the gods' purposes and beneficence."[146]

Several great aqueducts brought water into the city, and some of that water was used to furnish over a thousand public baths. These bathhouses were more than just places to bathe. "In addition to the exercise grounds, they contained promenades, gardens, libraries, restaurants, concert and lecture rooms, massage-rooms, and even rooms for medical men. Their outer walls were flanked by porticoes which were full of shops. The really large baths were civic centres; the smaller ones, community halls."[147]

All was not gorgeous, majestic, and lush, however. While numerous palaces were luxurious and many homes and apartments were roomy and comfortable and built around a central garden, "the hollows and valleys of Rome were crowded with tall tenements in which people were hived like bees or ants." The ground floor of these structures often housed shops or taverns, while the upper floors housed families, couples, and singles. These apartments were mostly one or two rooms in size, with the poorest renters on the highest floors. These buildings could go as high as eight stories, and they were built mostly of concrete, while the projecting balconies were composed of wood and brick. The staircases were made of stone or wood.

"Among those apartment and tenement blocks twisted about sixty miles of alleys and streets." Many of these lanes were just six feet wide. While there were a few thoroughfares fifteen to twenty feet wide, "ordinary streets were less than fifteen feet across." Most of the roadways were not paved, so muddy streets were common. And so were the smells. While Rome had a good sewage system and "elaborate public lavatories," the sewage system "did not reach, except in a few cases, beyond the ground floor. So, from the upper floors, slops were emptied into the street."[148]

Yet another problem in the city was "the constant noise and the continuous mobs pouring through the narrow thoroughfares." Julius Caesar (47–44 BC) had forbidden "wheeled traffic in Rome by day except for the carts of the building contractors." But what never stopped was foot traffic, and at night came "the rumbling of wagons and carts" and the talk and yells of drivers as "they brought in all the supplies the great city needed—vegetables, bricks, fish, meat on the hoof, marble, timbers, milk, and similar necessities." And because the streets were unlit, they invited "robbers and gangsters" to lurk in the darkness and search out unsuspecting prey.[149]

This was the city where Paul now took up residence as a captive.

- *Now finally in Rome, what turned out to be Paul's situation in captivity (v. 16)?*

- *After three days, whom did Paul ask to come to his residence, and what did he tell them about his reason for being in Rome and for gathering them together to hear him speak (vv. 17–20)?*

- *Had the Jews received any bad report about Paul? What were they eager to hear him talk about (vv. 21–22)?*

- *On another day, the prominent Jews met with Paul again, and this time an "even greater crowd gathered." What did Paul teach them, and from where did he build his arguments about Jesus (v. 23)?*

- *What were the responses from his audience (vv. 24–25)?*

- *What did their arguments prompt Paul to say to them (vv. 25–29)?*

- *For two-plus years, what was Paul's ongoing ministry in Rome (vv. 30–31)?*

The Rest of the Story

Paul's journey to Rome had taken six months (from August 59 to February 60).[150] And his residential incarceration lasted at least two years. Luke's book of Acts ends with Paul almost freely and unhindered proclaiming Jesus to Jew and gentile alike in the capital of the Roman Empire. The Twelve had begun this work in Jerusalem in AD 33, less than two months after Jesus' resurrection and ascension into heaven.[151] The good news had then spread to Judea, Samaria, Syria, Asia Minor, Macedonia, Greece, and other parts of the Mediterranean world—all of it empowered by the Spirit's work. Now the apostle Paul vocalized it in the political center of the Roman Empire. Jewish authorities had attempted to squash it, and gentile authorities had questioned it, found it curious, and decided it was not worthy of punishment. Nevertheless, Paul was allowed to perpetuate the gospel where the emperor lived and worked. The good news about Jesus was well on its way to being proclaimed throughout the world, at least the world that was known at that time. And all of this happened in about thirty years.

But was this the last word about the apostle Paul? What happened to the Jewish charges against him? Did he ever appear before the emperor Nero to plead his case? While Luke doesn't tell us, we have some information in other biblical texts and church history and tradition that allow us to provide some likely answers to these questions.

First, the Jewish case against Paul—what happened to it? The short answer is that no one knows for sure. What we do know is that the emperor Nero became less and less interested in his administrative duties as his time as emperor wore on. And one of the things he generally left for others to handle was judicial cases. His predecessor, Claudius, had taken measures to reduce his judicial caseload, and it's possible that Nero followed suit. There's also no indication in Acts that Paul's accusers in Palestine ever traveled to Rome to press their case against Paul. In fact, the Roman Jews told Paul that they had not received any communication from the Judean Jews about him, and they had not received a bad report about him from anyone (Acts 28:21). Assuming the Jewish prosecution never showed up in Rome to press their case, Nero or, more likely, someone serving in his judicial capacity may have simply dismissed the case and released Paul or heard Paul's defense and acquitted him.[152] Paul had expected to stand trial before the Roman emperor, and he also thought he would be released (Philippians 1:19–26; Philemon 22). Apparently, that's just what happened through Nero's designated proxy.

What, then, did Paul do? The testimony of a number of the church fathers is that Paul eventually made it all the way to Spain, the westernmost part of the Roman Empire.[153] In his letter to the Roman Christians, Paul had talked about his desire and plan to travel to Spain after spending time in Rome (Romans 15:24–29). At that juncture, he thought his trip to Rome would have been as a free man, not as a prisoner. Still, he made it to Rome—under guard. Then, sometime after his release, he traveled west to Spain as he wanted to do.

Several years later, Paul was arrested again (ca. AD 67), this time perhaps in Troas, and taken to Rome to stand trial. Paul "may have been taken by surprise since he had to request Timothy to go to Troas to pick up his cloak and scrolls (2 Tim. 4:13). That 2 Timothy records a second imprisonment is implied by a statement about Paul's 'first defense,' which resulted in his being 'delivered from the lion's mouth'" (4:16–18).[154]

Even before Paul's second arrest, the situation for Christians had become dangerous and deadly. In 64, a fire broke out in the poor section of Rome—the same place where Nero wanted to build his own palace and theme park. This fire destroyed or significantly damaged most of the sections of Rome. Nero was seen watching the fire and playing his lyre while the city burned. Rumors began to circulate that Nero had set the fire. To counter these, Nero blamed the Christians for what happened. Then he severely punished some of them by crucifixion and had others "sewn up in the skins of animals and hunted down by dogs," and still others were tied up to stakes, covered with pitch, and burned alive to serve as torches for Nero's private parties and to light up the city streets.[155] During this persecution, Nero had the apostle

Peter arrested and crucified. To escape this hostility against them, many Christians hid in the catacombs underneath the city.

Paul came into this situation to face a Nero already predisposed to finding Christians guilty of whatever they were charged with. Paul believed that this second imprisonment would end with his death. He told Timothy during this imprisonment, "The time is fast approaching for my release from this life and I am ready to be offered as a sacrifice" (2 Timothy 4:6). He urged Timothy to come to him quickly (v. 9). Paul knew his time on earth was coming to a close.

We know from church tradition that Paul was found guilty—of what charges, we do not know—and sentenced to death. He was then beheaded via a sword in a public execution. This occurred in the year 67 or 68.[156]

For Paul, his execution was not a defeat. While still imprisoned, he had told Timothy, "I have fought an excellent fight. I have finished my full course with all my might and I've kept my heart full of faith. There's a crown of righteousness waiting in heaven for me, and I know that my Lord will reward me on his day of righteous judgment. And this crown is not only waiting for me, but for all who love and long for his unveiling" (vv. 7–8). Paul had lived the life Christ wanted for him. He had been faithful to the end. With his part finished, Paul looked forward to all the reward, goodness, beauty, and fullness of life that Christ still had for him in heaven.

 EXPERIENCE GOD'S HEART

- *Why do you persevere in the Christian life? What or who keeps you going?*

- *Do you ever feel like giving up, even if just for a season? Why don't you give in to that? And if you have, do you find Paul's last written words to Timothy encouraging or inspiring? Why or why not?*

- *Following Christ can be costly, as the lives of the apostles demonstrate. But the rewards far outweigh that cost. Read Romans 8:18–39. Here Paul presents God's heart, provision, and promise for those of us who have committed ourselves to his Anointed One. What do you find there to help you keep on keeping on?*

 # SHARE GOD'S HEART

Sometimes we can become discouraged when people we share with or minister to do not respond favorably. Paul's typical strategy in such cases was to move on, to change his audience, not the essence of his message. He continued to proclaim Jesus and make his case for the gospel, but when his audience became hardened, he looked for softer hearts.

- *What are some telltale signs that someone's heart is hardened toward Jesus?*

- *How can you tell when someone's heart is more open to Christ?*

We may not be the ones whom an unbeliever will listen to. That's alright. Another Christian may make inroads that we could not. What matters most is that everyone has a chance to hear the good news about Jesus the Christ and choose whether they will put their faith in him. Some believers plant seeds in the field of unbelief, while other believers come along and water those seeds. But in all cases, it is God who causes the plants to take root and grow. And this occurs through those individuals who finally choose to trust in his Anointed One and center their lives on him.

- *Will you be a faithful messenger for Christ? Commit yourself to be this for him. Take time to do that now.*

Talking It Out

1. What takeaways did you have in this lesson or in previous ones that have begun to impact you the most?

2. What questions about the history of the early church did this study of Acts answer for you?

3. What questions do you still have about the church's early history?

4. After your study of Acts, what are your thoughts now about the role the Holy Spirit plays in the growth of Christ's church? In the ministries of his people?

Endnotes

1. Brian Simmons et al., "A Note to Readers," *The Passion Translation: The New Testament with Psalms, Proverbs, and Song of Songs* (Savage, MN: BroadStreet Publishing Group, 2020), ix.

2   For more evidence supporting Luke's authorship of Luke and Acts, see Donald Guthrie, *New Testament Introduction*, 4th ed. (Downers Grove, IL: InterVarsity Press, 1990), chs. 4 and 8; Darrell L. Bock, *Acts*, Baker Exegetical Commentary on the New Testament series (Grand Rapids, MI: Baker Academic, 2007), 15–24; Merrill C. Tenney, *New Testament Survey*, rev. ed. (Grand Rapids, MI: William B. Eerdmans, 1985), 176–79.

3   Paul L. Maier, *In the Fullness of Time: A Historian Looks at Christmas, Easter, and the Early Church* (New York: HarperCollins, 1991), 335–36.

4   F. F. Bruce, *New Testament History* (Garden City, NY: Anchor Books, 1969), 400–402.

5   R. N. Longenecker, "Paul, the Apostle," in *The Zondervan Pictorial Encyclopedia of the Bible*, 5 vols., ed. Merrill C. Tenney (Grand Rapids, MI: Zondervan, 1976), vol. 4, 654; B. Van Elderen, "Peter, Simon," in *The Zondervan Pictorial Encyclopedia of the Bible*, vol. 4, 738–39.

6   Richard L. Niswonger, *New Testament History* (Grand Rapids, MI: Zondervan, 1988), 267.

7   According to the Jewish historian and eyewitness Josephus, more than one million people in Jerusalem lost their lives. "Of those," he writes, "the largest number consisted of Jews by race, but not natives of Jerusalem; they had assembled from the whole country for the Feast of Unleavened Bread; and had suddenly been caught up in the war" (Josephus, *The Jewish War*, bk. 6, ch. 9, sec. 3). Some modern-day historians think Josephus's estimate is too high and put the number of people who died in the city closer to half a million or somewhat less. No matter the total number, the devastation upon the city and its temple was so great that it permanently altered the trajectory and practice of Judaism, and it forever shifted the heart of the new Christian movement from the center of Judaism to the larger gentile world.

8   For a discussion of when Jesus died, see Harold W. Hoehner, *Chronological Aspects of the Life of Christ* (Grand Rapids, MI: Zondervan, 1977), chs. 4 and 5. Bible scholars differ on what dates they assign to various events during Jesus' life and the later ministry work of the apostles. For the most part, we have followed Hoehner's chronological conclusions, realizing that other reputable scholars may differ with him occasionally but usually only by a year or two.

9   For more on the dating of Acts, see John A. T. Robinson, *Redating the New Testament* (Philadelphia, PA: Westminster Press, 1976), ch. 4; Guthrie, *New Testament Introduction*, 355–65; Stanely D. Toussaint, "Acts," *The Bible Knowledge Commentary: New Testament*, ed. John F. Walvoord and Roy B. Zuck (Wheaton, IL: Victor Books, 1983), 351–52; Richard N. Longenecker, "The Acts of the Apostles," *The Expositor's Bible Commentary*, gen. ed. Frank E. Gaebelein (Grand Rapids, MI: Zondervan, 1981), vol. 9, 235–38.

10 Robert H. Gundry, *A Survey of the New Testament*, rev. ed. (Grand Rapids, MI: Zondervan, 1981), 210.

11 For further substantiation of Luke's attention to historical detail, see F. F. Bruce, *The New Testament Documents: Are They Reliable?*, 5th ed. (Grand Rapids, MI: William B. Eerdmans, 1960), ch. 7. For an assessment of Luke as a historian, see I. Howard Marshall, *Luke: Historian and Theologian*, 3rd ed. (Downers Grove, IL: InterVarsity Press, 1988), chs. 1–3.

12 Acts, "Introduction," *The Passion Translation*, 2020 edition (Savage, MN: BroadStreet Publishing Group, 2020), 301.

13   Bock, *Acts*, 36.
14   Acts, "Introduction," TPT, 302.
15   Acts, "Introduction," TPT, 302.
16   Bock, *Acts*, 38.
17   Acts, "Introduction," TPT, 302.
18   Acts, "Introduction," TPT, 302.
19   Fritz Rienecker, *A Linguistic Key to the Greek New Testament*, trans. and ed. Cleon L. Rogers Jr. (Grand Rapids, MI: Zondervan, 1980), 758.
20   F. F. Bruce, *The Book of Acts*, The New International Commentary on the New Testament series (Grand Rapids, MI: William B. Eerdmans, 1981), 24.
21   Some recommended one-volume resources on church history are: Tim Dowley, ed., *Introduction to the History of Christianity*, 3rd ed. (Minneapolis, MN: Fortress Press, 2018); Owen Chadwick, *A History of Christianity* (New York: St. Martin's Press, 1995); Paul Johnson, *A History of Christianity* (New York: Macmillan, 1976); Earle E. Cairns, *Christianity through the Centuries: A History of the Christian Church*, 3rd ed. (Grand Rapids, MI: Zondervan, 1996); and, with a focus on the history of evangelism and missions, Ruth A. Tucker, *From Jerusalem to Irian Jaya: A Biographical History of Christian Missions*, 2nd ed. (Grand Rapids, MI: Zondervan, 2004).
22   Longenecker, "The Acts of the Apostles," 257.
23   New Testament scholar Harold Hoehner calculates the date of Jesus' ascension as May 14, 33. Hoehner also determines that Jesus was crucified on Friday, April 3, 33, and resurrected on Sunday, April 5. See his book *Chronological Aspects of the Life of Christ*, 143.
24   F. E. Hamilton, "Lots," in *The Zondervan Pictorial Encyclopedia of the Bible*, vol. 3, 988.
25   Bock, *Acts*, 90.
26   Bock, *Acts*, 95.
27   Hoehner, *Chronological Aspects of the Life of Christ*, 143.
28   To study what happened at Babel, see "Lesson 12: The Tower of Babel," in *TPT: The Book of Genesis—Part One: 12-Lesson Bible Study Guide* (Savage, MN: BroadStreet Publishing Group, 2022).
29   Longenecker, "The Acts of the Apostles," 301.
30   Bock, *Acts*, 186.
31   Eckhard J. Schnabel, *Acts*, Zondervan Exegetical Commentary Series, gen. ed. Clinton E. Arnold (Grand Rapids, MI: Zondervan, 2012), 233.
32   Schnabel, *Acts*, 233.
33   Longenecker, "The Acts of the Apostles," 301.
34   Longenecker, "The Acts of the Apostles," 301.
35   Bock, *Acts*, 189.
36   Longenecker, "The Acts of the Apostles," 302.
37   Schnabel, *Acts*, 236.
38   Acts 4:6, study note 'g,' TPT.
39   James D. G. Dunn, *The Acts of the Apostles* (Grand Rapids, MI: William B. Eerdmans, 1996), 63.
40   Schnabel, *Acts*, 285.
41   Schnabel, *Acts*, 288.
42   Harold Hoehner's dating of the apostolic era is presented in H. Wayne House, *Chronological and Background Charts of the New Testament* (Grand Rapids, MI: Zondervan, 1981), 129–32.
43   Josephus mentions a Theudas and his followers and their demise around AD 44, but this cannot be the same Theudas that Luke refers to. Luke's Theudas came before Judas the Galilean, and Judas' revolt occurred in AD 6. So this Theudas may have arisen after the death of King Herod the Great in 4 BC, for as New Testament scholar F. F. Bruce points out, "we know that many insurgent leaders arose in Palestine when Herod the Great died in 4 B.C., and Theudas may have been one of them" (Bruce, *The Book of Acts*, 125).
44   Bruce, *The Book of Acts*, 125.
45   Corey Piper, *500 Year Journey: From Babylon to Bethlehem* (New York: Morgan James, 2024), 81. For more on the census that led to this revolt, see in Piper's book, ch. 6; also "Lesson 1: The Prophet and the Savior," in *TPT: The Gospel of Luke: 12-Lesson*

46 *Bible Study Guide* (Savage, MN: BroadStreet Publishing Group, 2024).
46 Schnabel, *Acts*, 345.
47 Schnabel, *Acts*, 362.
48 Hoehner places Stephen's death in the year 35 (see House, *Chronological and Background Charts of the New Testament*, 129).
49 Mark L. Strauss, "Typological Geography and the Progress of the Gospel in Acts," in *Lexham Geographic Commentary on Acts through Revelation*, gen. ed. Barry J. Beitzel (Bellingham, WA: Lexham Press, 2019), 11.
50 Strauss, "Typological Geography and the Progress of the Gospel in Acts," 11.
51 Merrill F. Unger, *The New Unger's Bible Dictionary*, ed. R. K. Harrison (Chicago, IL: Moody Press, 1988), s.v. "Samaritans."
52 Justin Martyr, *First Apology of Justin*, ch. 26, in *Ante-Nicene Fathers*, vol. 1, ed. Alexander Roberts and James Donaldson (Peabody, MA: Hendrickson, 2004).
53 Irenaeus, *Against Heresies*, bk. 1, ch. 23, in *Ante-Nicene Fathers*, vol. 1, ed. Alexander Roberts and James Donaldson (Peabody, MA: Hendrickson, 2004).
54 Bock, *Acts*, 341.
55 Schnabel, *Acts*, 425–26.
56 Hoehner's dating, as found in House, *Chronological and Background Charts of the New Testament*, 129.
57 Schnabel, *Acts*, 441–42.
58 Unger, *The New Unger's Bible Dictionary*, s.v. "Lydda."
59 I. Howard Marshall, *Acts: An Introduction and Commentary*, vol. 5, Tyndale New Testament Commentaries, gen. ed. Leon Morris (Downers Grove, IL: InterVarsity Press, 1980), 189.
60 Marshall, *Acts*, 190.
61 Unger, *The New Unger's Bible Dictionary*, s.v. "Joppa."
62 Bock, *Acts*, 380.
63 Unger, *The New Unger's Bible Dictionary*, s.v. "Caesarea."
64 Bock, *Acts*, 385.
65 Bruce, *The Book of Acts*, 215.
66 Study note 'a' for Acts 10:48, TPT.
67 Bock, *Acts*, 412.
68 Bruce, *The Book of Acts*, 238. See also study note 'c' for Acts 11:20, TPT.
69 Larry W. Hurtado, *Destroyer of the Gods: Early Christian Distinctiveness in the Roman World* (Waco, TX: Baylor University Press, 2016), 94–95.
70 Bruce, *The Book of Acts*, 244.
71 Bruce, *The Book of Acts*, 244.
72 Longenecker, "The Acts of the Apostles," 407.
73 Longenecker, "The Acts of the Apostles," 407, 408.
74 Unger, *The New Unger's Bible Dictionary*, s.v. "James."
75 John's life, while still involving suffering for Christ (Revelation 1:9), ended differently than his brother's. John's death is not recorded in the New Testament, but early Christian tradition says that he was the last apostle to die, passing away "peacefully in Ephesus at an advanced age, around the year 100 A.D." (William Steuart McBirnie, *The Search for the Twelve Apostles* [Wheaton, IL: Tyndale House, 1973], 109).
76 John R. W. Stott, as quoted by Schnabel, *Acts*, 546.
77 Bruce, *The Book of Acts*, 257–58.
78 Schnabel, *Acts*, 554.
79 Schnabel, *Acts*, 554.
80 Schnabel, *Acts*, 554.
81 Schnabel, *Acts*, 557.
82 Bock, *Acts*, 450.
83 Josephus, as cited in Bock, *Acts*, 450–51.
84 Bock, *Acts*, 451.
85 Schnabel, *Acts*, 603.
86 Schnabel, *Acts*, 605.
87 If you would like to learn more about worldviews, here are some valuable resources: Norman L. Geisler and William D. Watkins, *Worlds Apart: A Handbook on World Views*, 2nd ed. (Eugene, OR: Wipf and Stock, 1989); James W. Sire, *Naming the Elephant:*

Worldview as a Concept, 2nd ed. (Downers Grove, IL: InterVarsity Press, 2015); James W. Sire, *The Universe Next Door: A Basic Worldview Catalog*, 6th ed. (Downers Grove, IL: InterVarsity Press, 2020); Kenneth Richard Samples, *A World of Difference: Putting Christian Truth-Claims to the Worldview Test* (Grand Rapids, MI: Baker Books, 2007).

88   Hoehner's dating, as found in House, *Chronological and Background Charts of the New Testament*, 129.

89   The actual decisions made by each of the seven major church councils after the one held in Jerusalem (Acts 15) can be found in volume 14, *The Seven Ecumenical Councils*, ed. Henry R. Percival, of the *Nicene and Post-Nicene Fathers*, second series, ed. Philip Schaff and Henry Wace (Peabody, MA: Hendrickson, 1994).

90   For still more on Silas, see TPT, Acts 15:40, study note 'd.'

91   F. F. Bruce, *The Pauline Circle* (Grand Rapids, MI: William B. Eerdmans, 1985), 24.

92   Bruce, *The Pauline Circle*, 28.

93   Bruce, *The Pauline Circle*, 29–30.

94   Bock, *Acts*, 528.

95   Bock, *Acts*, 533.

96   Schnabel, *Acts*, 703.

97   Bock, *Acts*, 550.

98   Bock, *Acts*, 553.

99   See Longenecker, "The Acts of the Apostles," 470; and Schnabel, *Acts*, 209.

100   Bock, *Acts*, 555; TPT, Acts 17:10, note 'b.'

101   Longenecker, "The Acts of the Apostles," 473.

102   Longenecker, "The Acts of the Apostles," 474.

103   F. F. Bruce, *Jesus and Paul: Places They Knew* (Nashville, TN: Thomas Nelson, 1981), 99–100.

104   Bock, *Acts*, 577.

105   Toussaint, "Acts," *The Bible Knowledge Commentary*, 405.

106   David K. Lowery, "1 Corinthians," *The Bible Knowledge Commentary*, 505.

107   Bruce, *Jesus and Paul*, 101, 104.

108   Bruce, *Jesus and Paul*, 103.

109   Hoehner's dating, as found in House, *Chronological and Background Charts of the New Testament*, 130.

110   Hoehner's dating, as found in House, *Chronological and Background Charts of the New Testament*, 130–31. To follow Paul's journey, see the map titled "Paul's Third Missionary Journey" in TPT.

111   Bruce, *The Book of Acts*, 379–80.

112   Bock, *Acts*, 605.

113   Longenecker, "The Acts of the Apostles," 500.

114   Bock, *Acts*, 605.

115   This chart is a slightly modified version of the one found in Schnabel, *Acts*, 827.

116   Schnabel, *Acts*, 874.

117   Schnabel, *Acts*, 876.

118   Schnabel, *Acts*, 892.

119   Schnabel, *Acts*, 926.

120   Hoehner's dating, as found in House, *Chronological and Background Charts of the New Testament*, 131.

121   Unger, *The New Unger's Bible Dictionary*, s.v. "Felix."

122   Paul H. Wright, "The Geography of Caesarea Maritima," in *Lexham Geographic Commentary on Acts through Revelation*, 216.

123   Schnabel, *Acts*, 968.

124   E. M. Blaiklock, "Festus, Porcius," in *The Zondervan Pictorial Encyclopedia of the Bible*, vol. 2, 533.

125   Longenecker, "The Acts of the Apostles," 545.

126   Hoehner's dating, as found in House, *Chronological and Background Charts of the New Testament*, 131.

127   Longenecker, "The Acts of the Apostles," 546.

128   H. W. Hoehner, "Herod," in *The Zondervan Pictorial Encyclopedia of the Bible*, vol. 3, 144.

129   See, for example, Douglas Groothuis, *Christian Apologetics: A Comprehensive Case*

for *Biblical Faith*, 2nd ed. (Downers Grove, IL: InterVarsity Press, 2022); Norman L. Geisler and Frank Turek, *I Don't Have Enough Faith to Be an Atheist* (Wheaton, IL: Crossway Books, 2004); Kenneth Richard Samples, *Without a Doubt: Answering the 20 Toughest Faith Questions* (Grand Rapids, MI: Baker Books, 2004); Lee Strobel, *The Case for Faith: A Journalist Investigates the Toughest Objections to Christianity* (Grand Rapids, MI: Zondervan, 2000); J. Warner Wallace, *Cold-Case Christianity*, updated ed. (Colorado Springs, CO: David C. Cook, 2023).

130   To follow Paul's trip to Rome, see the map titled "Paul's Journey to Rome" in TPT.
131   Longenecker, "The Acts of the Apostles," 558.
132   Longenecker, "The Acts of the Apostles," 558.
133   Longenecker, "The Acts of the Apostles," 558.
134   Schnabel, *Acts*, 1034.
135   Longenecker, "The Acts of the Apostles," 558.
136   Longenecker, "The Acts of the Apostles," 558.
137   Longenecker, "The Acts of the Apostles," 559.
138   Longenecker, "The Acts of the Apostles," 563.
139   Longenecker, "The Acts of the Apostles," 564.
140   Bruce, *Jesus and Paul*, 120.
141   Seutonius, as quoted by Gary R. Habermas, *The Verdict of History* (Eastbourne, England: Monarch Publications, 1988), 94.
142   Bruce, *Jesus and Paul*, 125.
143   Bruce, *The Book of Acts*, 531.
144   David A. DeSilva, "The Social and Geographical World of Rome," in *Lexham Geographic Commentary on Acts through Revelation*, 432.
145   Lesley Adkins and Roy A. Adkins, *Handbook to Life in Ancient Rome* (New York: Oxford University Press, 1994), 272, 262.
146   DeSilva, "The Social and Geographical World of Rome," 433–34.
147   W. G. Hardy, *The Greek and Roman World*, rev. ed. (Cambridge, MA: Schenkman Publishing, 1970), 88.
148   Hardy, *The Greek and Roman World*, 90.
149   Hardy, *The Greek and Roman World*, 90.
150   Hoehner's dating, as found in House, *Chronological and Background Charts of the New Testament*, 131.
151   See Hoehner, *Chronological Aspects of the Life of Christ*, 143.
152   For a more extensive discussion on this judicial matter with Paul, see A. N. White, *Roman Society and Roman Law in the New Testament* (Grand Rapids, MI: Baker Book House, 1963), 108–119.
153   McBirnie quotes from Clement (a disciple of Paul and later bishop of Rome; see Philippians 4:3), the third century church historian Eusebius (who cites Chrysostom and Jerome), and the fourth century Bible scholar Jerome who declare that Paul's first imprisonment ended in his release and subsequent missionary travel to the far western part of the empire, Spain (see McBirnie, *The Search for the Twelve Apostles*, 282–83).
154   Niswonger, *New Testament History*, 256.
155   Bruce, *New Testament History*, 401.
156   In 68, the emperor Nero met his end. The Roman legions conspired to assassinate him. Galbo, the governor of the Spanish provinces, led a revolt against him. Nero's guards abandoned him, the Roman senate declared him to be an outlaw, and a Roman guard tried to kill him. Nero finally committed suicide. See Michael Grant, *The Twelve Caesars* (New York: Barnes & Noble, 1996), 171–73.